RAILROAD PATHFINDER

THE LIFE AND TIMES OF

Edward L. Berthoud

RAILROAD PATHFINDER

THE LIFE AND TIMES OF

Edward L. Berthoud

ROBERT C. BLACK III

CORDILLERA PRESS, INC.

Publishers in the Rockies

Copyright 1988 by Robert C. Black III

Library of Congress Cataloging-in-Publication Data

Black, Robert C., 1914
    Railroad pathfinder : the life and times of Edward L. Berthoud /
Robert C. Black III.
        p.   cm.
    Bibliography: p.
    Includes index.
    ISBN 0-917895-24-X
    1. Berthoud, Edward L. 2. Explorers — Colorado — Biography. 3. Railroads
— Colorado — History — 19th century. 4. Colorado — Surveys — History —
19th century. 5. Railroad engineers — Colorado — History — 19th century.
I. Title.
F781.B47B58 1988
978.8'02'0924 — dc 19
[B]   88-30226
                                                                              CIP

First Printing

    1   2   3   4   5   6   7   8   9

Printed in the United States of America.

Cover Painting
    Edward Berthoud's career was closely tied to Clear Creek Canyon, which is depicted here
    in Colorado artist John E. Green's acrylic painting of No. 71. Green has combined his love
    of trains and painting in earnest in recent years and his works have been shown throughout
    Colorado, in Taos and Santa Fe, and in Los Angeles, as well as being published in books
    and magazines.

Cover Design
    Richard M. Kohen, Shadow Canyon Graphics

Design & Typography
    Shadow Canyon Graphics   Evergreen, Colorado

Cordillera Press, Inc.   Post Office Box 3699   Evergreen, Colorado 80439.   (303) 670-3010.

CONTENTS

ACKNOWLEDGEMENTS

Edward Louis Berthoud deserves a better historical press. His identity is nowadays quite uncertain, even in his Rocky Mountain West. Nationally, he is almost unknown. His name is recalled chiefly by skiers, who remember — sometimes imprecisely — a mountain crossing. Even the considerable literature of the Colorado continental divide accords him less than moderate attention. Certain of his references are altogether inaccurate; for example, Berthoud was not a Swiss engineer, brought in directly from the Alps to create an American St. Gotthard.

On the other hand, the average researcher seldom encounters a subject that has never, ever, been examined before. Even Edward Berthoud has received a few polite nods. Yet there is only a single piece about him that can properly be called a biography, and this remains sequestered in typescript. I therefore hope that this present book will help to reduce a deficiency.

Information on Berthoud is widely scattered, and I consequently find myself owing thanks to large numbers of individuals and organizations. There are in fact so many that I am obligated to severely compress my gratitude.

A major place for the study of Berthoud and his times is the library of the Colorado Historical Society in Denver. Another is the Western History Department of the Denver Public Library. Mrs. Kay Engel has been the principal custodian for Berthoud in the first, Mrs. Eleanor Gehres in the second. Both have helped me enormously.

Data upon Berthoud's boyhood and youth are chiefly to be found in Montgomery County, New York, where Mrs. Ruth V. Lupo, historian of the Town of Palatine, has been an indispensable guide. Much of the flavor of his young manhood, on the other hand, is to be found in a single title in the library of the New York Historical Society in New York City, a remarkable private memoir by Silas Wright Burt, Berthoud's most intimate college friend.

Next come the great repositories, of which the New York Public Library, the National Archives system, and the Library of Congress are representative. All have afforded me handsome dividends. The same may be said, in a more specialized sense, of the unique Latter Day Saints Family History Library in Salt Lake City.

Other facilities are to be classed as lesser only in the matter of size. We encounter here the vaults of county clerks — those at Golden, Colorado, and Independence, Missouri, in particular. There are likewise the multifarious state and local historical societies and associations: the Kansas State Historical Society in Topeka, where Larry Jochims and Maxine Benson cooperated with effectiveness and dispatch; the municipal collections at Golden; the Mason County Museum at Maysville, Kentucky, where Molly Kendall combined graciousness with efficiency; and the Grand County Museum in Hot Sulphur Springs, Colorado, which conveniently embraces a high percentage of my personal friends. The Colorado Railroad Museum and Bob Richardson and the Geological Museum of the Colorado School of Mines cannot be left out, nor can the Missouri Valley Room of the Kansas City Public Library. A very special repository no longer exists, the Porter Library of the former Colorado Women's College, but I can still convey my affectionate thanks to my faculty colleagues there — Faye Carey, Paul Frame, and Arleen Ahern.

Certain specialized materials were available at Fort Larned Historic Site, Kansas, and in the Cavalry Museum at Fort Riley. Both collections cleared up some awkward details of Berthoud's Civil War activities. In Missouri, at Warrensburg, the admirable library and museums of the Johnson County Historical Society nicely re-created the background of his unusual activities from July 1864, to January 1865. At Independence, Mrs. Donald B. Ehrlich of the Jackson County Historical Society provided welcome assistance with the problems created — for Berthoud and almost everyone else — by General Ewing's Order Number Eleven. There is also, at Jefferson City, the very special historic area called Jefferson Landing, where Bill Fannin provided an enthusiastic commentary upon the Confederate operations of October 1864, and a personally inscribed map that saved this study from some appalling tactical errors!

At Cordillera Press, my principal guides and friends have been Walt Borneman and Jay Fell. Of these gentlemen I can only say that it is a pleasure to be associated with them and that I greatly appreciate their high technical standards and, especially, instinct for railroads.

Finally, I must offer my thanks to Maxine Benson, major historian of both Colorado and Kansas, who first recommended Edward Berthoud as a promising subject for study. I furthermore must ask her pardon for the distressingly long period of time that has elapsed between her suggestion and the completion of this book. For this I alone am responsible.

Robert C. Black III
Sky Valley Ranch
Tabernash, Colorado
May 8, 1988

For my children,
who know Berthoud's pass
so well.

INTRODUCTION

For four turbulent decades, Edward L. Berthoud was the quintessential righthand man to Western railroad enterprise. After cutting his teeth as a civil engineer on the disease-ridden pioneer line across the Isthmus of Panama, Berthoud moved west with the tide of North American development. Working competently — and often confidentially — with such promoters as Thomas Ewing, W.A.H. Loveland, and the highly controversial Jay Gould, Berthoud surveyed a number of the routes which would convert paper railroads into functioning networks.

Edward Berthoud's 1861 exploration of the Colorado mountain pass that bears his name was but his first major involvement with efforts to build a railroad directly west through the Southern Rockies. As an adviser to the inner circle of politicians and businessmen who sought to make Golden, Colorado, preeminent over rival Denver, he assisted with experimental links to the Kansas Pacific and the Union Pacific. Later, he surveyed and helped direct the construction of the Colorado Central Railroad, not only from Golden into Wyoming, but also to Central City and Georgetown.

Jay Gould's interest in the Colorado Central led Berthoud into additional engineering assignments in other portions of Gould's empire, but Berthoud always called Golden home and continued to be involved with efforts to overcome the Colorado continental divide, including the famed Georgetown Loop.

Berthoud was seldom the leader, but always the able and trusted associate. His life offers keen insight into the bitter politics and physical challenges of nineteenth-century railroading in the Rocky Mountain West.

CHAPTER I

The Making of an Engineer

Berthoud is a surname that is seldom enountered in the United States. It is quite absent from any standard reference works, and it is widely known only in the State of Colorado. Even there, it designates few living persons, and in a recent directory for the Denver area it refers only to a mountain pass, an incorporated town, and a collegiate building. The pass is not a gateway of the very first importance, although it does excel, in terms of scenery, many of those that are. Berthoud, the town, is a pleasant community with a noble outlook; nowadays it faces urban engulfment. Berthoud Hall is of dignified aspect, a principal unit of the Colorado School of Mines. Pass, town, and building commemorate a Colorado pioneer of whom the world at large has taken only moderate notice.[1]

Yet the Berthoud name, so sparse in America, is frequent enough in parts of the Old World. With slight variations, it occurs in the Lower Valais, in Brittany, Flanders, Brabant, Picardy, and Santonge. It is found most often, however, in the folds of the Jura Mountains. No less than five Berthoud coats of arms have emerged from the Canton of Neuchâtel, a principality of ancient identity that for centuries has served the Swiss as their northwest frontier. Indeed, the name has been so special to this region that its French-speaking inhabitants have found it convenient to refer to Germanic Burgdorf, in adjacent Canton Bern, as "Berthoud."[2]

The disposition of many young Swiss to wander over Europe in quest of opportunity is well known. It was a Helvetian couple of this sort that became the parents, in London in 1787, of a son named Charles Louis Henri Berthoud. The child flourished exceedingly, received an international education, and ultimately attained a physical height, unusual for the time, of more than six feet. While still in his early twenties, he served with pride as a finance officer in the armies of the first Napoleon. He emerged from this experience with a pronounced military bearing — "straight as a candle" — and with a lifelong reluctance to discuss the outcome of Waterloo. Of his three given names, he favored Louis.[3]

Immediately following the fall of Napoleon, this vigorous young man married a youthful *Vaudoise* of Lausanne named Louise Haupt and embarked with pronounced energy upon a mercantile career. His new interests soon carried him, with his wife, rather far afield, and their first recorded children, Margaret and Frederic Stephen, were born in New York City. By 1820, they had returned to Europe and for more than a decade resided in the venerable city of Geneva, where Louis Berthoud prospered and Louise bore four additional children, Matilde, Emilie, Alexandre Pierre, and on March 29, 1828, Eduard Louis. It was this youngest son who would leave the Berthoud name on the pass, the town, and the hall.[4]

Geneva in the later 1820s was what it has basically remained, a mildly dour place, French in speech, but never quite in habit, yet grandly situated at the foot of one of the world's loveliest lakes. It was not, however, to be a significant influence upon the youngest Berthoud, for his father, still in his prime and scenting advantage, chose suddenly to set out again with his family on the tedious and still perilous journey to the New World. Aboard an unremembered vessel, they slipped into New York harbor upon an autumn tide in 1830. Little Eduard was only two, and already his memories of Lac Léman and the distant snows of Mont Blanc were fast fading away.[5]

New York in the early 1830s was in the midst of its most auspicious era; already it was surpassing Mexico City as the most populous center in the Americas. It was not yet a metropolis, however, but was contained within the chin of Manhattan Island. *Longworth's City Directory* was issued in easily portable *quarto* size. Indeed, for New York, the nineteenth century had scarcely begun. Its municipal odors continued redolent of the 1700s, and as late as 1832, an outbreak of cholera would inspire the publication of a hasty map that purported to prove that the disease did not spread. At the time of the Berthouds' arrival, no steam locomotive had as yet entered the city. But Manhattan's chin was heavily bearded with masts, side-wheel steamboats churned through an incomparable complex of protected waterways, and the city's alleys were raucous with the cries of draymen. Year by year, *Longworth* thickened.[6]

Such was the environment that began the Americanization of Eduard Berthoud. First, there was the matter of language. Although his parents were already fluent in an accented English, his mother tongue was undoutedly French. (Indeed, certain Gallicisms were to accompany him through life.) An early and perfect acquisition of American speech was nevertheless inevitable. Eduard was young, and he enjoyed, by virtue of his birth, the mysterious continental aptitude for languages, while everywhere in the adjacent streets there resounded the abrasive English of New York, that most stubborn of all dialects in its refusal to cater to the convenience of foreigners.[7]

In fact, his family already had discovered the Anglo-American inability to pronounce "Bare-too", which was "Berthoud" as rendered in the lands of its origin. They presently substituted a penultimately accented "*Bir*-thew" and clung to it, with slight success, for many years. As late as 1861, the youngest Berthoud suggested "*Ber*-thude" as a workable compromise. Even this was ineffective. Hardly had his Colorado pass appeared upon the maps than it became "*Burr*-th'd", which to the American ear seemed entirely reasonable.[8]

American practice was equally unwilling to concede the use of Gallic given names. In due course, Eduard became "Edward." It was likewise inevitable that Louis should often be converted orally to "Lewis," and occasionally, by outsiders, it was so spelled. These adjustments were probably accepted with resignation, for it is clear that the Berthouds intended this move to America to be permanent.[9]

In any case, Edward's father was presently listed, in New World style, in Mr. Longworth's directory as "Charles L. Berthoud, merchant," with a place of business at 408 Greenwich Street. The premises doubtless served also as the family residence because any separate domicile would have been specified. The building stood close to the intersection of Greenwich and Hubert streets in a district that represented the 1831 equivalent of "midtown." The structure probably violated every modern canon of habitability, but by the standards of the day it enjoyed a prestigious location. To the east, up Greenwich Street, St. John's Park afforded greenery; to the west, the Hudson River revealed itself with gliding schooners.[10]

The precise nature of Mr. Berthoud's activities is obscure, although subsequent facts suggest they were successful. We do know that two additional Berthouds, Nicholas and Ernest, were in the city during the 1830s and early 1840s and that they were importers. They may have been relatives, but neither was an associate. Moreover, "Charles L." abruptly left New York with his wife and children in the latter part of 1832.[11]

It was his final move, and somewhat difficult to explain. To abandon New York, whose preeminence already was guaranteed, in favor of a Mohawk valley village seemed out of character. Certainly Louis was not driven by difficult circumstances. His new neighbors whispered of a forty-thousand-dollar fortune, and it was public knowledge that he had paid three-thousand dollars, cash, for John Fickel's farm. The cholera may have been a factor; it continued to lurk a scant half-dozen blocks from Greenwich Street.[12]

Perhaps it was a simple matter of taste. The list of those who have rejected lower Manhattan for a rural retreat is endless. Furthermore, his new establishment was by no means trivial. The farm embraced 225 elm-dotted acres and was regarded as one of the most attractive properties in the Town of Palatine Bridge. Nor was it really isolated. The Mohawk valley was in fact a corridor of national importance, indispensable to the canal boats that underwrote the supremacy of New York. Mr. Berthoud's land was bounded on one side by the Mohawk River itself. On the opposite bank, across a sturdy new bridge, rose the spires of Fort Plain. Upriver, past massive escarpments, the continent began.[13]

Life in such a milieu cannot have been wholly dull. It was furthermore distinctly American. Regional echoes of the Netherlands and Germany were confined by now to proper names. Although the elder Berthoud occasionally worked his land with his own hands, he remained primarily an entrepreneur, trading acres, acquiring mortgages, and, beginning in the mid-1830s, platting a hamlet. Local expectations ran high. In 1834, following complicated negotiations, men with rods and tripods appeared on the river bank and soon were followed by sweating battalions of laborers. Whether Edward, aged six, was especially impressed by the surveyors is doubtful, but he probably stood entranced, when, at the age of eight, the first train of the Utica & Schenectady Railroad drew its pillar of smoke through the valley. From that day forward, the steam locomotive would beat out one of the basic rhythms of his life.[14]

The family farmhouse survives, though nowadays much modified. Built of dressed stone, it was one and one-half stories high and featured a central living room with an enormous fireplace. It was a sturdy ediface and well suited to the local climate, which, according to season, might be Arctic or tropic. It trembled only slightly from the rumblings of the primitive passenger trains.[15]

Like a good many boys of his time and place, Edward Louis Berthoud received a surprisingly good basic education. Much of it derived from a sophisticated family, but it was effectively supplemented in a rough cabin "up the gully" and later in the public school across the river in Fort Plain. The latter was reckoned, even then, a fire-trap and lacked certain of the requisites of an "academy," but it turned out a surprising number of serious scholars. Among Berthoud's schoolmates were a certain Diefendorf, who would accompany him to college, and a much younger boy, Lucien W. Bliss, whom he would later encounter, under bizarre circumstances, at the foot of the Rocky Mountains.

Fort Plain likewise offered places of worship, and the Berthouds associated themselves first with the local Reformed Church and later with the Methodists. Although most of his family sought godly fellowship "by profession," young Edward did not. Time would demonstrate that he was by no means irreligious, but he would always exhibit a curious disinclination to accept confirmed membership in any Christian body.[16]

Meanwhile, he grew toward manhood. "Edward" long since had turned, under village pressure, to "Ed" or "Ned". Although he failed by many inches to equal his father's stature, he did inherit his father's posture and throughout life held his five and one-half feet perfectly straight. As a youth he could rightly be called "skinny," but this characteristic soon evolved into a happy tendency not to put on weight. He became wiry and superbly adapted to withstand physical hardship. He furthermore enjoyed a marked capacity for good health. He was never quite handsome — a lengthy nose forbade it. Nor was he notably gregarious. He was seldom at ease in a crowd, and, in common with

Union College at Schenectady, New York, in 1842, shortly before Berthoud matriculated to study engineering. *Courtesy of the New York Historical Society, New York City.*

his father, he loathed confrontations with the vulgar. His eyes were of the palest blue, yet very keen, and they looked out upon the world with unfeigned curiosity, though not always with admiration. He was in no way an aesthete. Physically, he was intended for frontiers, mentally for the sciences.[17]

In the autumn of 1845, when he still was seventeen, Ed Berthoud traveled forty miles down the Mohawk to enter Union College at Schenectady. It was hardly a plunge into the unknown. His older brother, Alexander, had preceded him by five years and as an undergraduate had become a principal founder of Chi Psi, a secret society with a considerable destiny. In addition, Alexander had been attracted to the technical aspects of the curriculum, areas in which Union was already a pioneer, and had graduated Phi Beta Kappa.[18]

In many respects, young Berthoud simply followed in his brother's footsteps. He was initiated into Chi Psi; he devoured technical courses; and he was received in his senior year into the Phi Beta Kappa Society. Of his fellow students he would always remember Chester Alan Arthur, who entered Union College that same autumn as a sophomore and who quickly became noted for his sociability and, especially, his flamboyant attire — attributes that he would eventually carry into the presidency of the United States. Berthoud was even better acquainted with Frederick W. Seward, the talented son of a major alumnus, William Henry Seward, who already was reaching for the political stars. But his closest friend at Union was Silas Wright Burt, a well-favored youth from Kinderhook, New York, and who, like Berthoud, sought scientific pursuits and joined Chi Psi.[19]

Union's facilities, though rather sparse, possessed a certain dignity. Two buildings, painted gray and white, the work of the gifted architect Joseph Jacques Ramée, marked the easterly perimeter of a carefully platted quadrangle. To the north, a botanical garden, arranged according to Linnaean standards, afforded relaxation and an opportunity for the systematic observation of flora and fauna. The college's most remarkable object, however, was its president, the Reverend Eliphalet Nott, a long-nosed New Englander without an earned degree, who was perhaps the ablest American educator of his generation.[20]

Nott had been president of Union since 1804, and he would leave the office only in death in 1866, at the age of 93. His final senility was prodigious (in Berthoud's time it was foreshadowed by a crippling arthritis), but in 1845, he was still renowned as an innovator. Nott was a liberal in the authentic sense. In his admissions policies, he welcomed so many of the expelled of other institutions that Union became known as "Botany Bay." As to curriculum, undergraduates were assumed to be gentlemen, and their lives were singularly free from petty restraints and obligations. Nott was also a patriot. He endorsed a Jacksonian brand of nationalism, and urged, though with indifferent results, the admission of Southerners to his college. His campus seldom was disrupted by the excesses of the antislavery movement. His enthusiasm for his institution was total. His presidential letterhead was adorned with buildings that had not yet been built, and he was so avid a fund-raiser as to provoke an undercurrent of student suspicion and, in Albany, of official criticism. [21]

Edward Berthoud, class of 1849, readily absorbed the predilections of Eliphalet Nott's college. Indeed, they simply confirmed his own. He appears not to have resented unduly the Spartan facilities of West College, a half-derelict dormitory a full mile from the principal campus, to which most of the resident underclassmen were consigned. He promptly elected to follow a brand-new intensive in engineering, a program that was unique in a liberal arts school. Although respected by his classmates, he was manifestly not a leader. He did participate in venial exploits — one episode, perfected by Silas Burt, featured a parody of divine service in a long-advertised but as yet non-existent college chapel. His sole significant unhappiness was occasioned by the death of his mother in the spring of his freshman year.[22]

The educational process can seem endless to a young man, but the day at last came (it was July 25) when "Old Prex" Nott donned his traditional three-cornered hat to bestow diplomas upon the class of 1849. Edward Louis Berthoud received an arts degree in engineering, which was not really an anomaly, for Union took care to build its technical innovations upon a liberal arts base. His precise rank in his class is unknown, but it must have been close to the top, for he achieved Phi Beta Kappa status (automatic for the upper third) without question. Silas Burt, also an engineering major, nearly missed such honors, "owing," he claimed , "to the unreasonable animosity of Professor Reed."[23]

Neither Burt nor Berthoud nor the majority of the graduating seniors appear to have taken serious notice of the war with Mexico, which their college years had encompassed and which now had rounded out, and simultaneously divided, the United States. It had broken out in Texas in the spring of their freshman year and was officially over while they still were juniors. As an adventure in imperialism it had been only thinly disguised, but its immediate yield was handsome — a whole new American southwest, very much larger than the old one. Yet it triggered instant discord, specifically the question of black slavery within arid spaces previously called free, and the entire Union College Class of 1849 had presently to face it.

At Union College in Berthoud's time, President Nott served as his own director of placement, and it was his habit to provide members of the senior class with letters of recommendation, drawn up by a secretary and signed in his quavery, arthritic scrawl. Berthoud received his letter as early as January 8; it attested to his "unblemished character," referred to his "high stand as a scholar," and pronounced him "worthy of confidence and esteem." Nevertheless, the young man and especially his father sought something more than a routine accolade, and even before Nott drew up his recommendation, the elder Berthoud wrote from Fort Plain to no less personage than the celebrated novelist, James Fenimore Cooper, seeking assistance for his son in securing an appointment as a United States Army topographical engineer. How and when the Berthouds had made the acquaintance of so eminent an individual is uncertain, but they evidently were far from strangers, for Cooper wrote at once, in his own hand, a most flattering letter of introduction, addressed to General Winfield Scott, which the younger Berthoud appears to have carried, full of expectation, to Washington. Alas, the endorsements of Nott and Cooper were insufficient to assure such a position. By the summer of 1849, the federal military was in the midst of one of its postwar disintegrations, and Ed Berthoud's first postgraduate employment turned out to be an extension of a summer vacation position he recently had held with the Morris Canal Company in New Jersey.[24]

This was not, as a matter of fact, a job to be scoffed at. The canal company was a considerable organization, and its superintendent, William Hubbard Talcott, was a practical engineer of exceptional talent. Service under such a man afforded the best kind of experience. Moreover, Talcott respected Berthoud as only one who is competent but undereducated can respect another who, though formally trained, is without presumption.

Together they faced rigorous problems. The Morris Canal had been intended as a short cut for anthracite coal and pig iron between Phillipsburg, New Jersey, on the Delaware River, and the westerly reaches of New York harbor. This meant crossing the grain of northern New Jersey, a formidable succession of forested ridges, at one point reaching an elevation of 914 feet above sea level. This involved the use of inclined planes, devices which, if not unprecedented, were inherently experimental. The original canal had been completed — after a fashion — as early as 1832, but it had proved too light for effective use and was now, following an obligatory financial reorganization, being rebuilt on a much heavier scale. Throughout 1850 and into 1851, Berthoud toiled over the leafy slopes, adjusting track, improvising hoists, and installing new patterns of cable. He gave much satisfaction: he was temperate, diligent and efficient, and he completed his stint with the rank of assistant engineer in full charge of one of the planes. "He has acquired a good knowledge of practical mechanics," wrote Talcott with a certain pride, "beyond what is usual in an engineer." The canal, when reopened, paid dividends for over two decades. Berthoud, for his part, never forgot the excellent Talcott, or the possibilities of inclined planes.[25]

At the conclusion of his employment with the Morris Canal, the young man found himself in the City of New York and in a mood for something venturesome. He had not long to wait. The recent acquisition of California and the almost simultaneous discovery of gold there had inspired one of the major treasure hunts of history. Already it had peppered the sea with ships, including experimental steam packets, that undertook to convey passengers and priority freight to selected isthmian crossings, of which the state of Panama in the Republic of Nueva Granada offered the shortest land transit. Panama was also, of course, a natural invitation for a railroad.

By the spring of 1851, a "Panama Rail Road Company," with principal offices in New York, was already in existence and was advertising vigorously for trained civil engineers. Its terms of employment were, by contemporary standards, princely: a starting salary of $100.00 per month, with board, lodging, medical attendance, and round-trip passage from New York provided by the company. (Likewise available, though unmentioned, was complimentary burial in Panama.) On April 21, 1851, Ed Berthoud accepted, on these conditions, an appointment as an assistant civil engineer. He was aboard the next company steamer when it cleared Sandy Hook five days later.[26]

For more than a week, the ship plowed through warming seas, shaking to the thrust of its experimental engines. Toward the last there were glimpses of high islands and finally, to the south, a barrier of rounded hills, well forested and oddly suggestive of a skyline in upstate New York. The hills were still in the distance when the vessel cast anchor and Berthoud and a push of other passengers were taken ashore by lighter. There they encountered, not upstate New York, but a tropical horror.

The Panama Railroad, as originally laid out, followed generally the peculiar northwest to southeast course of the later ship canal from the Caribbean to the Pacific. This was, in 1851, a relatively new route; it did not conform very closely to the classic *Camino Real*, and it sought initially to take advantage, by means of shallow-draft steamboats, of the lower course of the Rio Chagres. It did reduce the traditional mule track by more than one-half and furthermore offered the lowest summit crossing in many miles. But for a railroad and its terminal facilities, the Atlantic shore imposed severe difficulties, in particular a large morass, saturated by the effluence of the Rio Mindi, that interposed itself between suitable wharfage sites and the solid ground of the isthmus proper.[27]

Berthoud was assigned to this swamp. It was everything repelling that a Latin American *ciénaga* could be. It was virtually bottomless; it emanated offensive odors; and it served as home for a variety of appalling life forms. To force a five-foot-gauge railroad across it required heroic measures, including the deliberate engulfment of entire train-loads of rock. The task occupied many months, in the course of which a large percentage of the company's work force — black, oriental, and caucasian — died. Malaria and yellow fever undoubtedly played a part, but the primary killer was cholera, a swift and virulent strain that dispatched its victims, in agony, within hours. To work in such an environment was fundamentally suicidal; nevertheless, the personal ability of Edward Berthoud not to become ill proved effective against nearly everything the area could muster. He did suffer briefly from a fever (it was provisionally diagnosed as yellow), but thereafter the lithe little engineer kept steadily on his feet, while those around him dropped by the hundreds.[28]

Berthoud asserted many years later that life in Panama had been "a veritable hell on earth". Yet even this pesthole had its compensations. As a very junior officer, Berthoud was fortunate to work under the supervision of two remarkable men: George M. Totten, the company's chief engineer, and Totten's principal deputy, James L. Baldwin. Totten's career, often as a designer of fortifications, has been widely noted, but we would like to know more of Baldwin, for he obviously became a major influence in shaping Berthoud's special character. Baldwin was a born naturalist. He was unabashedly fascinated by the isthmian flora and fauna, appalling or not. Berthoud, who had found bemuse-ment in the labeled preserve at Union College, quickly perceived a kindred spirit, and it was inevitable that the two should devote their leisure hours to the examination of palms and ceibas, monkeys and macaws. Berthoud became especially engrossed with the avifauna. He was delighted by the seasonal passages of a North American swallow (probably the cliff swallow), and he carefully recorded the unexpected abundance, in June 1852, of a local species which he somewhat cavalierly dubbed a "Woodcock."[29]

Near the end of 1851, the morass was at least subdued, and Baldwin and Berthoud were reassigned to firmer ground along the right bank of the Chagres.[30] Neither was involved with locating the line; that task had been completed some time previously, and they found themselves confined to such homely details as culverts and abutments. They appear not to have worked together so closely as before, and Berthoud sometimes found himself nearly alone. His isolation deepened as the rainy season of 1852 became established, for it brought sickness and death to even this better drained region. From May through July he labored between downpours at a wretched river-bluff village called Frijola and watched forty-six of his 240 laborers die. Many more of the survivors were carried away to hospital ships. By midsummer Berthoud and a Scottish mess steward were "the only valid white men left at Frijola," while beneath their feet the swelling river bore seaward a floatsam of trees, snakes, and cadavers.[31]

The formal statistics were staggering. It is recorded that the greater part of Totten's technical staff, fifty-one engineers, surveyors, and draftsmen, lost their lives that summer; Totten, Baldwin, and Berthoud appear to have been the principal survivors. Indeed, the Panama Railroad became so short-handed that Berthoud was put in charge of the operation of trains between Gatun Station and the end of iron. For a time he found himself responsible for shipments of gold and the still increasing throngs of gold seekers. The latter were supplemented late in July by eight companies of the 4th Regiment of United States Infantry, enroute to posts on the new American Pacific coast. In immediate charge of their transit was an acting quartermaster, a slim young officer named Ulysses S. Grant, brevet captain of the Mexican War, who contrived to maintain a basic discipline in the face of nearly impossible odds. That Grant enountered Berthoud is likely, though undocumented. We know only that the military fatalities, chiefly from cholera, approached eighty men.[32]

Berthoud by this time had had enough of Panama. Because the railroad company imposed a rigorous salary deduction upon any employee who cut short a minimum service period of six months, he was careful not to depart until his final stint was completed in October 1852. In the meantime, he participated in the planning for a permanent bridge over the Chagres and helped to stake out the famous crossing of the continental divide at Culebra Hill. Although his resistance to disease had been phenomenal, the company steamer did not deliver him to New York wholly untouched. Thanks to the deficiencies of his

Panamanian diet he had lived for months on the fringes of scurvy, and though he appears never to have become totally incapacitated, he came ashore in a distinctly weakened condition. A lifetime of rewarding activity awaited him, but it is notable that he thereafter kept meticulously away from the raw tropics. [33]

His recuperation, however, was rapid. He dabbled for a season in real estate at Palatine Bridge, but accomplished little. He was attracted inexorably elsewhere; the entire United States seemed suddenly to be calling for civil engineers. The nation was deep in its first major overindulgence in railroad building, and early in the following spring (1853) Ed Berthoud once again found himself in the employ of a railroad company. [34]

This latest enterprise proposed to build a line of five-foot gauge from Maysville, Kentucky, on the Ohio River, to Lexington, the well-known "capital" of the Blue Grass country. The undertaking enjoyed an interesting background as it included a segment of the ancient "trace" between Zanesville, Ohio, and Natchez, Mississippi, and represented a reincarnation in iron of the controversial turnpike that a famous Jacksonian veto had thwarted twenty-three years before. In charge of the venture as chief engineer was a gifted Anglo-Irishman named Neil Macneale. [35]

Ed Berthoud, with the title of assistant engineer, was placed upon the first division of the road, with headquarters at Maysville, and once more he found himself among stimulating associates. Macneale was another practical genius, trained in the great English railway mania of the early 1840s. Ruddy-faced and slender, he towered physically over Berthoud. Though deeply religious, he was marked by a curiously irreverent sense of humor, and he delighted in poking fun at the pretensions of metaphysicians. Responsibility for the second portion of the line was in the hands of A.G. "Al" Whiton, one of Berthoud's Union classmates. Whether this association was coincidental, or whether they had sought employment together, is uncertain. [36]

Work upon the Maysville & Lexington was both fascinating and rigorous. The Ohio valley at Maysville was like the Mohawk valley at Fort Plain — its sides rose abruptly in wooded steps, while the plateau beyond was intricately dissected by the numerous tributaries of the Licking River. Even Macneale was pushed to the limits of his abilities, while for Berthoud and Whiton it was a relentless and valuable training

The Lee House at Maysville, Kentucky, a center of activity when Berthoud worked on the Maysville & Lexington Railroad in the early 1850s. *Courtesy of Robert C. Black, III.*

exercise.[37]

One afternoon in mid-April, 1853, the high professional atmosphere was turned suddenly hilarious by the appearance of a third Union alumnus, none other than Berthoud's old intimate, Silas Wright Burt. So happy a development naturally suggested celebration, and it is known that the three friends drank deeply that evening of the contents of a large brown jug. We are futhermore informed that they were rescued from oblivion the following morning by a grinning young black with a pitcher of "sick water," a river-front preparation of obscure formula but with remarkable healing powers. Though faintly nauseous, it enabled the youthful engineers to resume their duties almost at once.[38]

Burt had come downriver from Pittsburgh in the role of general con-tractor, with the intention of bidding upon the new Maysville rail terminal, but his arrival produced unexpected trouble. None of the trio appears to have been greatly disturbed by the habits of a slave-hold-

Book traces achievements of mystery man Berthoud

Railroad Pathfinder: The Life and Times of Edward L. Berthoud
By Robert C. Black, III.
Cordillera Press of Evergreen. 176 pages.
$10.95.

Daily Books

By TOM NOEL

Berthoud Pass, Berthoud own and Berthoud Hall at the Colorado School of Mines commemorate a mystery man.

Edward Louis Henry Berthoud, a Swiss engineer of encyclopedic interests and accomplishments, attracted Robert C. Black's attention because he "had never, ever, been examined before." Few of the lionized characters of Colorado history laid broader or more useful foundations than the modest man quietly put to rest in 1908 Golden Cemetery.

Berthoud came to Colorado in 1860 and surveyed Berthoud Pass the next year for the "Colorado and Pacific" toll road that evolved into U.S. 40. He was speaker of the house in the 1866 Colorado Territorial legislature, where his moderate, democratic politics soon caused him to be demoted to Territorial Librarian.

Berthoud also wrote history — *The Rocky Mountain Gold Regions,* a crackerjack 1861 overview of the history, geography, botany, geology, mines and businesses of Colorado.

Berthoud gave much to the Colorado School of Mines, where he taught and was a trustee. In Golden, he served as mayor and as a Jefferson County commissioner. He surveyed the Denver, Lakewood and Golden Interurban line and the Colorado Central Railroad.

Tom Noel, an associate professor of history and director of Colorado Studies at CU-Denver, teaches and writes about Colorado history.

Experiencing and

After drugs and alcohol, dre

By MIKE PEARSON
News Staff Writer

The life of Merry Lynn Noble reads like something from the pages of the *National Enquirer* or a pulp science fiction novel.

It's the sort of story that makes you wonder if truth is indeed stranger than fiction or if, after awhile, fiction *becomes* truth.

But whether or not you believe what Noble has to say, you can't deny that she believes in her 1982 experience.

Raised in an atheistic family on a farm in northern Montana, Noble, now 40, fled an abusive home at age 18 for Denver. She attended college and succumbed to alcohol and drugs, and soon after became a prostitute. For five years she plied her trade in New York, Los Angeles and Denver, searching, she says, for a sense of

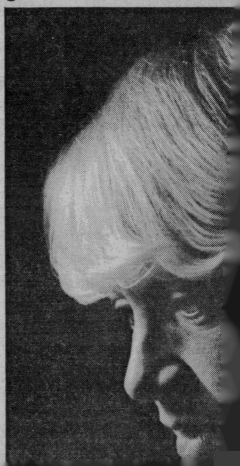

ing community; their college had stressed moderation in such matters, and Berthoud and Whiton as professionally trained employees had encountered no unpleasantness. But with Burt it was different; he was quickly perceived as an overweening Yankee, competitive with local enterprise. Within a day or so there was murmuring in the streets and carefully drawled threats. That night Berthoud quietly rowed his chum out into the river and thrust him aboard a passing steamboat.[39]

Despite the optimistic business climate, the Maysville & Lexington was not fortunate in its balance sheets. The venerable "trace" had lost its federal patronage in 1830, and during the 1840s the State of Kentucky had rejected further commitment to railroad subsidies. The notion of public assistance did linger on the municipal level, and fairly substantial sums were pledged by the city of Maysville and the counties of Fayette and Bourbon. Although a provisional half-dozen miles was opened with ceremonies at Maysville in October 1853, and although trains were running from Lexington to Paris before the end of the same year, local resources were not enough. It was perhaps prophetic that both termini of the little road had been established in graveyards, for the company soon found itself unable to meet its operating expenses. The local service from Maysville was canceled, the Lexington stub leased, and bankruptcy proceedings intitiated. The graveyards would not be linked by rail until 1868.[40]

The collapse of the Maysville & Lexington quite naturally deprived Berthoud and his collegues of their jobs. Whiton drifted into a New York office, while Macneale secured a position with a fledgling railroad in Tennessee. Berthoud's movements became obscure. A short biographical sketch, published with his cooperation in 1881, makes casual mention of activities in "Kentucky, Ohio, Indiana, Wisconsin and Iowa," but there is firm information only for Kentucky and Indiana. (Indeed, the sources for Edward L. Berthoud leave a good deal to be desired. He eschewed diary-keeping and habitually neglected to preserve his private correspondence. Aside from a short reminiscence or two, he published nothing of an autobiographical nature. He remains a challenge to any researcher.)[41]

For the Kentucky and Indiana episodes we are indebted chiefly to Silas Burt, who did keep diaries and who later converted them into several large volumes of handwritten memoirs. It should be remembered that Burt was a trained engineer; in fact, he consistently surpassed

Berthoud in the neatness though not always in the accuracy of his work. One of his earlier positions, contemporaneous with Berthoud's period in Panama, had been with the Great Western Railway in Canada West (now Ontario), and there he had encountered one John M. Ferrell, a bluff but thoroughly competent railroad contractor from upstate New York. Mr. Ferrell had two daughters, and with the younger, Nettie, aged fifteen, Silas Burt fell hopelessly in love. Thereafter, as Nettie matured, Burt repeatedly sought employment as close as possible to the shifting locations of the Ferrell family.[42]

Early in 1854, Silas met with some incredibly good luck. Mr. Ferrell was currently involved in some extensive grading along the Wabash valley for the Lake Erie, Wabash & Western Railroad, with headquarters in Logansport, Indiana, and Burt contrived to secure a position as division engineer on the Logansport & Northern Indiana, a complementary carrier with offices in the same city. Indeed, he presently got himself a cozy berth with the Wabash company itself, and as his successor on the L. & N. I. he suggested Berthoud.[43]

The post was proffered and accepted. Berthoud for the moment was at loose ends, and he furthermore was permitted to bring with him as his assistant another old acquaintance, William E. McCormick, Chi Psi, Union, 1850. Everyone was delighted: "The great congregation of engineers at Logansport made everything in business and society quite lively," Burt later recalled, and when Neil Macneale suddenly offered Berthoud a rather better position in Tennessee, the latter — for an increasingly good reason — chose to remain in Indiana. Macneale did write him a generous letter of recommendation: "I consider him," he asserted, "a gentleman and one who is a good engineer."[44]

Berthoud truly enjoyed Logansport. It was a bustling place, an established river and canal center given additional vitality as an emerging railroad junction. Sited at the confluence of the Eel and Wabash Rivers, it already was much more than a county seat. The two valleys traced complementary routes from Lake Erie toward the Mississippi, and L.S. Nash, chief engineer of the Logansport & Northern Indiana, already had issued a suggestive map depicting his unfinished railroad as an indispensable element in the mainstream of American commerce. Meanwhile the grading of the Wabash was being pushed with energy, and the little coterie of junior engineers continued to enjoy a season of satisfying effort and pleasant conviviality. The latter would be

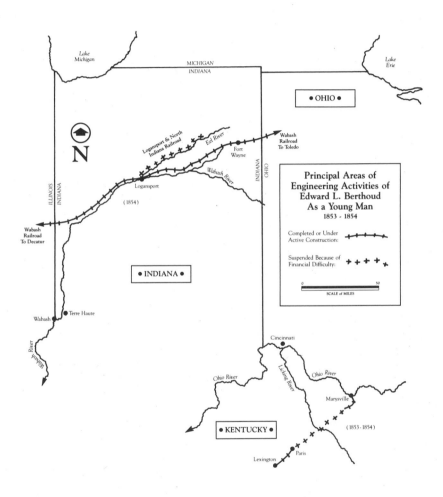

Principal Areas of
Engineering Activities of
Edward L. Berthoud
As a Young Man
1853 - 1854

climaxed by the formal engagement of Silas Burt and Nettie Ferrell. [45]

There was, in the end, a single difficulty — money. (It is instructive to discover how many hopeful railroad schemes met with heavy financial weather in the midst of the prosperous 1850s.) Berthoud and McCormick might stake their tangents beside the River Eel, but they were followed by neither graders nor rails. Even the Wabash company was obligated to meet its bills with dubious scrip, and well before the end of 1854 it was evident that the Logansport & Northern Indiana had foundered absolutely. Once again Berthoud was out of work. [46]

Yet Logansport had been by no means a waste of effort, for it was here that he became acquainted with the Ferrells. They were a distinctly varied family. John M. Ferrell combined the vivid speech of a muleskinner with a profound absorption in the Episcopal Church — he currently dominated the local parish. His wife, Jeannette, was an impeccable housekeeper and an inspired cook. Their sons, Frank and Charles, were conventional. Of their two daughters the younger, Nettie, was now the intended of Silas Burt. It was the elder who became, for Berthoud, of central importance. [47]

Her name was Helen Samaria. By her family and friends she was called — invariably — "Samaria." Born in central New York in 1830, she had participated in most of her father's peregrinations, yet had achieved, under a variety of circumstances, a surprisingly sound formal education. Thanks to a hopeless scattering of family photographs, her appearance cannot be recalled, but of her admirable qualities there can be no question. The surviving data strongly suggest that she was Edward Berthoud's first authentic love, and it is altogether certain that she was his last. In any case, before the end of 1854 their friendship had proceeded to a private understanding. [48]

Berthoud, alas, could not remain in Logansport, nor could he contemplate early marriage. The Logansport & Northern Indiana continued in its slough of despondency. He may have served very briefly in a series of "spot" positions across the middle west, and there are indications that his father was induced to pay certain of his expenses. He had not yet, to be truthful, risen very far, either professionally or financially. But he had undergone major seasoning, and he furthermore had established a useful tendency, which was to follow instinctively the westward thrust of American development. [49]

CHAPTER II

The West Begins

As late as 1850, the western boundary of Missouri marked an authentic frontier. Within the state, the land was "settled," with a mixed agriculture, ranges of townships, tiers of counties, and well-defined rights of private property. But beyond the state limits there were no settlements in the usual sense — no counties, no local laws, and no order other than that within rifle shot of certain widely scattered military posts. Here, for more than two decades, the west, in its more primitive aspects, began.

One factor in this situation was the presence, on "permanent" reservations, of considerable numbers of Indians, many of them agricultural and semi-sedentary. But of far greater consequence was the national inability to agree upon the rules for the westward extension of slavery. No enabling legislation for the establishment of civil authority in the regions beyond Missouri would emerge from Washington until the passage of the Kansas-Nebraska Act in May 1854. But when at last this happened, it set off a veritable explosion of settlement, enhanced by land-lust long repressed, and it carried Ed Berthoud with it to the newly organized Territory of Kansas in the early spring of 1855. He traveled in vast discomfort, impacted among fellow emigrants aboard a Missouri River stern-wheeler, the first of the season. There were several available destinations, all of them close to the new territorial limits: Westport Landing, Leavenworth, Atchison, and St. Joseph. Berthoud, for reasons unspecified, chose Leavenworth.[1]

Leavenworth, Kansas, was still very new; the long-established Fort

Leavenworth, though adjacent, was separate. But the town was spreading over its neighboring bluffs, and litters of steamboats, snouts upstream, nuzzled its levee. Within a year its population had doubled, generating municipal needs. The opportunities for a trained engineer were obvious.[2]

Leavenworth was also tense. It was a proving ground for emerging social patterns, and it was coveted by two major factions, pro and anti-slavery, neither of them disposed to compromise with the other. To be sure, Leavenworth would never suffer so grievously from guerrilla warfare as did Lawrence and the Wakarusa valley, and it is safe to assume that the greater proportion of its newcomers had arrived in quest of simple economic advantage. Their outlook was specifically catered-to by Leavenworth's famous Planters' House, which drew a kind of Mason's and Dixon's Line across its barroom floor and employed a corps of impartial bounders to eject those who failed to respect it. Nonetheless, unpleasantness did erupt — and occasionally it reached serious proportions.[3]

Berthoud must be listed among the simple seekers of fortune. His career to date — in particular his college years — had confirmed his natural moderation. He harbored no brief for slavery, but neither was he disposed to disrupt a community by insisting upon its instant abolition. As the future would repeatedly demonstrate, he was not a political animal.

His initial activities in Leavenworth escape us. But late in July he signed a contract with the General Land Office — it was the eighth to be concluded in Kansas Territory — to run township lines. This was a fundamental procedure, without which sections, quarter-sections and formal entries would be impossible. It was, technically speaking, a straightforward process, conducted across a moderately rolling mosaic of prairie and hardwood. But in the relentless heat of the mid-western summer it could be rigorous. Sickness plagued nearly every field party that season, and as late as November only fifty of the 145 authorized townships had been fully enclosed. Berthoud himself did not submit his final report until December 17, but his unit did ultimately establish more than 108 miles of line. His remuneration from the land office came to $703.98.[4]

Nor was the experience wholly unpleasant. In September his assignment carried him to the headwaters of the Grasshopper (Delaware)

River, close to certain villages of Kickapoo Indians, and he promptly undertook, part-time, to study their intricate language. This was unusual behavior in a contract surveyor, and the Indians were immensely pleased. They recently had been compressed into the southwestern corner of their traditional reservation and were understandably grateful for any sort of sympathy. Indeed, young Mr. Berthoud became a kind of tradition among them, a legend that developed over the years until, a half-century later, he would be recognized as a major advocate of Kickapoo interests in three states.

Although we may suppose that heat-prostrated rodmen were a factor in Berthoud's tardiness, we may suspect that there were other elements. He was so easily distracted! The Kickapoo linguistics are a case in point; moreover, it was inevitable that he should become fascinated by the regional flora and fauna. The Missouri valley not only drained the north and west, but also afforded an avenue to numerous species from the east and south. The woodland groves were consequently rich in arboreal variety, and their prairie fringes supported myriads of cardinals, "mockers," and other birds. Berthoud took special pleasure in the green and saffron flutterings of the Carolina parakeet, a doomed breed of North American parrot that was still of frequent occurrence. There were also some strictly professional deviations. We find evidence of a short-lived real estate promotion called the Helena Association, the sort of thing that would be deemed a conflict of interest nowadays, but not in 1855. Moreover, on September 11, in the very midst of his land office responsibilities, he accepted an appointment as city engineer of Leavenworth![5]

He did anticipate an indefinite, perhaps permanent, commitment to Kansas, and in the mild February of 1856 he journeyed to Logansport to be united in marriage with Helen Samaria Ferrell. No specific record of the ceremony survives other than in his own handwriting in his French family Bible. The couple would remain childless. It was nevertheless a conspicuously successful match; indeed, it would one day be likened to a "domestic poem." But from the start the groom refused to cope with his bride's usual given name, and "Samaria" quickly became "Helen."[6]

Berthoud performed no further work for the land office in Kansas and he resigned, following major misunderstandings with the municipal council, his position as city engineer in the autumn of 1857. But he was seldom without employment. Already he had entered into an association with yet another railroad scheme. It was called the Leavenworth, Pawneee & Western, and its immediate purpose was to engross for Leavenworth the principal commerce of the valley of the Kansas River. This meant effective control of much of the territory. As a major tributary of the Missouri, the Kansas River thrust a woodland finger deep into the prairies for more than a hundred miles, and near its tip lay Fort Riley, an already well-established army post. Close to Fort Riley, moreover, stood "Pawnee City," a massive stone warehouse with considerable expectations, both economic and political. The river, though officially navigable, was frequently not, and beyond the fingertip its several forks led on and on into the west, toward possibilities that as yet could only be imagined. It was the kind of situation that inevitably bred a railroad, swaddled in paper.[7]

The project enjoyed a distinguished sponsorship. Conspicuous among its directors were Hugh and Thomas Ewing, young Ohioans of genteel background who had opened a law office on Main Street immediately above the mayor's chambers. The Ewings were by no means enthusiastic for slavery, but were — at this point — of such moderate disposition that they got on famously with many of those who were, including the widely-known jurist, Samuel D. Lecompte. When their foster brother — and brother-in-law — a former regular army officer named William Tecumseh Sherman, sought to join their firm, Lecompte saw to it that Sherman received an immediate license to practice on "grounds of general intelligence." Already the Ewings had induced the judge to serve as provisional president of their railroad. Furthermore, their own "free-state" proclivities might render them effective advocates, before a Northern-dominated House of Representatives, for a federal land grant.[8]

Berthoud, whose credentials were impeccable and political passions nil, was an obvious choice for the company's field work. He set out in May 1857 and submitted his profiles before the end of the year. His line contoured the prairie swells from Leavenworth to a point on the Kansas River directly opposite of the "free-soil" city of Lawrence, thence followed a water grade along the north bank to a terminus beneath the bluff at Fort Riley. This arrangement would present an obstacle to any effort of newly established Kansas City to dominate the valley. Indeed, it set off a public dickering and bickering that grew

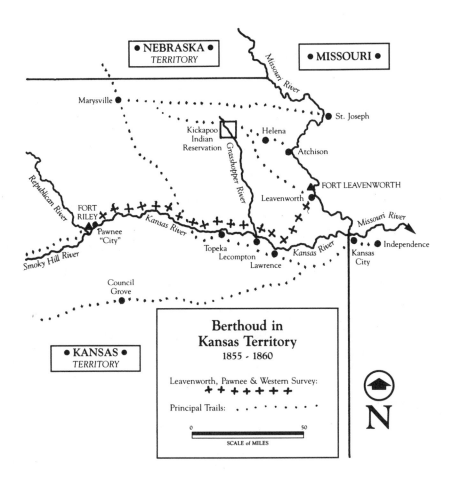

NEBRASKA
TERRITORY

MISSOURI

Missouri River

Marysville

St. Joseph

Kickapoo
Indian
Reservation

Helena

Grasshopper River

Atchison

Republican River

FORT
RILEY

FORT LEAVENWORTH

Leavenworth

Kansas River

Missouri River

Pawnee
"City"

Smoky Hill River

Topeka
Lecompton
Lawrence

Kansas River

Kansas
City

Independence

Council
Grove

KANSAS
TERRITORY

**Berthoud in
Kansas Territory**
1855 - 1860

Leavenworth, Pawnee & Western Survey:
+ + + + + + +

Principal Trails: . . . .

0   50

SCALE of MILES

N

to national prominence two years later with the Wyandotte Constitutional Convention. Of the discord Berthoud took little notice, nor was he disturbed when a lack of funds — and of federal sympathy — precluded immediate grading. He did take pains, however, to record the presence of the Carolina parakeet along the entire Kansas valley. Moreover, his association with the Ewings continued; their character, in such a community, as educated men assured it. He grew closest to the affable Thomas, whose legal concerns embraced the Kickapoo Indians, and their acquaintance would lead during the Civil War to an interesting practical consequence.[9]

Berthoud may not have been able to keep entirely clear of the regional rough-stuff. Leavenworth faced across a common river the slave-holding state of Missouri, and the actively pro-slavery segment of its population was in consequence rather strong. Late in the summer of 1856, this element organized a vigilance committee which, on September 1, undertook to expel all suspected "free-soilers" from the community. About a third of the citizenry was thereupon hustled aboard a collection of river craft and cut adrift. That Berthoud was a victim is unclear, but certain surviving statistics indicate that one of the ejectees was of Swiss birth. The tatterdemalion "regulators" remained in effective control for months, but most of the abducted soon returned to their homes. There were rumors of pillage, but Berthoud later recalled that the Missourians were "more intent on political ostracism than material plundering."[10]

Berthoud and Helen continued to think of Leavenworth as home, and before the end of 1857 they were joined by her parents, who faced sudden and unexpected destitution as a consequence of the "railroad panic" of that year. In the course of the following spring there also appeared the Ferrell boys, Charles and Frank. All of them combined their resources to lease and refit the Shawnee House, a hostelry potentially of the genteel class that occupied a "pleasant and healthy" site within a few rods of the great brick pile of the Planter's House. Their efforts were successful, and the Shawnee soon acquired a reputation and clientele of unquestioned respectability; indeed, numerous marriages were solemnized in its parlors. Its quiet prosperity kept the Ferrells afloat and enabled the Berthouds to maintain a modest but comfortable residence at the corner of Third and Osage streets. In addition, Ed kept a private office at 60 Main Street, in close proximity

to the Ewings, from which, in association with one Beebe, he conducted an engineering, surveying, and land agent's business. A catastrophic fire in July 1858 left them all unscathed. There even was
another Berthoud in Kansas. Ed's brother, Stephen, had become a
leading citizen of the village of Louisville in Pottawatomie County.[11]

But Leavenworth was not to be lifelong. Five hundred miles to the
west, close beneath the Rocky Mountains, a party of migratory prospectors had encountered obvious signs of gold, and the news reached
Leavenworth shortly after the fire. This, given the contemporary tendency to overlook cost economics, set off a "rush," a sudden eruption
of private, frequently individual, enterprise, thoughtless alike of reality
and of environmental impact. It quickly drew Leavenworth into a kind
of magnetic field — the town afforded perhaps the closest approach
by dependable steam navigation to the new bonanza. Before the end
of 1858, the local papers were crowded with a new kind of advertising:
"Ho! for Pike's Peak! Outfitters to the Emigrant! Every necessity for
crossing the Plains! Try us!" (Pikes Peak, it turned out, rose at some
distance from the initial gold strikes.)[12]

The effect upon many people was irresistible. John Ferrell, who had
responded to booms all his working life, was swept westward in the
spring of 1859, together with his wife and sons. The Berthouds — at
first — stayed put. The mania had brought a renewed bustle to Leavenworth itself; once again (and despite a heavy loss of its earlier population) the place doubled in size. By the middle of 1859, it had become
a city of 10,000 people, allegedly the largest between St. Louis and
San Francisco. Yet Berthoud, too, felt the magnetism. Within days he
readied a sketch map of the plains, which soon appeared in lithograph
as "A Map of Routes to the Gold Region of Western Kansas." Compiled
chiefly from official data, it was easy to read and reasonably accurate. In
1859, he resurveyed in greater detail the Pawnee railroad and even
expanded his professional reputation with an imaginary branch office
in the new settlement of "Denver City, Western Kansas," which he
ventured to insert in two successive issues of the Leavenworth city
directory.[13]

For nearly two years, young Mr. Berthoud assumed an uncertain
posture with one foot in Leavenworth and a potential foot in the
shadow of the Rockies. Leavenworth — and especially the Ewings —
tried hard to keep him; late in the winter of 1860 there were proposals

for a wagon road that would serve as a temporary substitute for the railroad, not only to Fort Riley and "Pike's Peak," but beyond via the "parks" to the Great Salt Lake. Furthermore, on March 10, the city council tendered him $500 in municipal warrants in return for "surveying and making a route from Ft. Riley to Denver City, on the condition that Mr. Berthoud give bond for faithful performance of the work." There followed a spate of public meetings and editorial urgings.[14]

Berthoud, however, gave no bond; instead, he left Leavenworth. The Pikes Peak temptation had grown too strong, and he and Helen were off for the mountains in mid-March 1860. Although he may have flattered himself that his departure involved no dereliction of duty, he did experience some qualms, and many months later would admit to Thomas Ewing that his behavior had been "inauspicious."[15]

Their chosen desination was not Denver, but an infant settlement at the immediate foot of the mountains called Golden City, where the Ferrells had established, amid promising indications, a toll bridge (over present Clear Creek) and a hotel. The manner of their travel is not positively known, though there are hints of a four-mule wagon and an overall party of fifty. Berthoud as usual kept no regular diary. It is reasonable, however, to suppose that they followed the classic route across country to Fort Kearney, thence up the Platte, and its southerly fork. We do know that the weather and the "going" were remarkably good and that on the evening of March 23 an exquisite crescent moon hung above the western horizon close to a brilliant planet, Venus. Berthoud did record their entry — beyond Fort Kearney — into a semi-arid world, but not of their first breathtaking views of the Rockies. This was normal. He would always treat mountains as a scientist, less in awe than in curiosity. If he stood silent before them it was to consider how and of what substance they were made, with what living things they were associated, and most of all, how best they might be crossed. They arrived in Golden City on April 18, 1860. Although Ed and Helen could not know it then, they had come home.[16]

*   *   *

The Ferrells were waiting — John and Jeannette, and perhaps the boys. Golden City was a crude place. Less than a year old, it had a population, preponderately male and youthful, of less than 1,000. Its

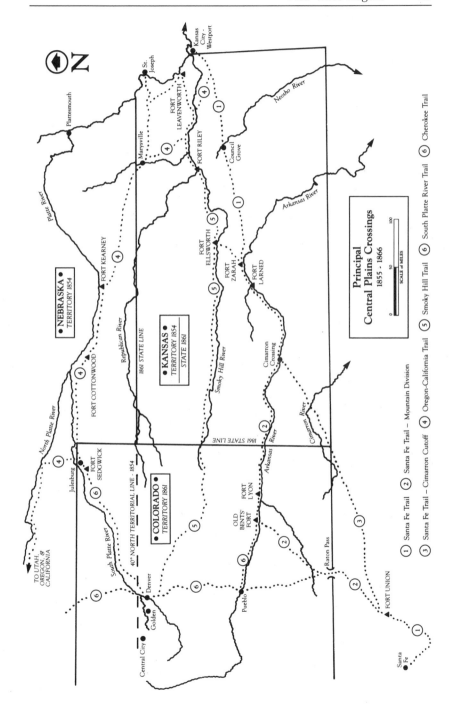

Principal
Central Plains Crossings
1855 - 1866

① Santa Fe Trail ② Santa Fe Trail – Mountain Division
③ Santa Fe Trail – Cimarron Cutoff ④ Oregon-California Trail ⑤ Smoky Hill Trail ⑥ South Platte River Trail

① Santa Fe Trail ② Santa Fe Trail – Cimarron Cutoff ④ Oregon-California Trail ⑤ Smoky Hill Trail ⑥ Cherokee Trail primitive buildings stood unprotected beneath the western glare; to the east rose two stark tablelands, while westward there loomed the bare initial rampart of the Rockies. Hardly had the Berthouds arrived when the landscape was plastered with unseasonable snows. John Ferrell was nevertheless fairly bursting with enthusiasm. His bridge was yielding revenue; his hotel — a slab-sided building called the Miner's House — was being doubled in size; he was conspicuous in regional politics; he was dreaming of a ranch; and he already was revered as a founding father. His wife, moreover, kept the best kitchen west of the Missouri River. [17]

The Berthouds responded suitably. Helen joined her mother in the kitchen; Ed undertook a sweeping reconnaissance. He fairly devoured the locale, evaluating its topography and recording, with an appealing naiveté, its flora and fauna. The fauna included, inevitably, the Carolina parakeet. Following a circumvention of canyons, he pitched a fragile tent among the placers of North Clear Creek and proffered his technical services. [18]

These undertakings were clearly provisional. Shortly before his departure from Leavenworth, Berthoud had invited his old fraternity brother and brother-in-law, Silas Wright Burt, to join him as a partner, not only in civil engineering, but in the vending of mining and smelting apparatus. Burt responded with enthusiasm. Forsaking a small empire of iron furnaces in the hills of eastern New York, he departed for the Rockies at the first sign of spring, taking with him his wife and a cluster of mechanics. All were in Golden by May 20. Burt enjoyed the journey immensely. Like Berthoud, he fancied himself a "natural philosopher;" furthermore, unlike Berthoud, he was a gifted delineator, and he arrived in Golden with a collection of exquisite sketches, depicting plants, animals, and his fellow travelers, plus a delicate rendering of the Rockies as viewed from the plains on a brilliant spring morning. [19]

The Burts and the Berthouds established themselves in a wing of the Ferrell's hotel, cheek by jowl with a coal miner, a lawyer, and a teamster. Nettie joined Helen in the kitchen; their husbands embarked, in the fashion of tenderfeet, upon the awesome program of activity. They platted a southern addition to Golden City — in the course of which they mistook a standing prairie dog for a survey stake. They measured, without significant accuracy, the elevation of South Table

Mountain, and they completed, with increasing precision, the triangulation of a score of additional stations. To the north of town they ran
the bounds of Mr. Ferrell's dream ranch, dubbed "Manito's Throne."
For a fee, they analyzed the regional minerals. They examined the
canyon of Clear Creek as a possible railroad route. They mused over
Indian vestiges. They gathered mining data. They contemplated the
political scene, in particular the so-called Territory of Jefferson and its
provisional Jefferson County. They were amused to discover that the
territorial secretary, and occasional acting governor, was Lucien Wood
Bliss, aged 27, who Berthoud rememberd as a very young pupil at the
Fort Plain public school. Bliss had been the victorious participant in
a recent duel with shotguns, and Burt, though no physician, had
occasion to examine his mortally shattered victim.[20]

It was all unquestionably fascinating, yet Silas Burt became progres-
sively more disillusioned with the "Pike's Peak" Eldorado. His Dutchess
County ironmongers made indifferent prospectors. His vaunted "caloric
engines" failed to perform. A letter from no less a personage than
Horace Greeley suggested, in flat contravention of legend, that the
Rocky Mountain West faced an uncertain future. But the principal
difficulty was psychological. Unlike Ed and Helen Berthoud, Silas and
Nettie Burt simply lacked the instinct to remain in so uncouth a
community. By mid-September, they had decided to depart, and on
October 18 they boarded the stage for St. Joseph. The Ferrells and
Helen, but not Ed, went to Denver to bid them good-bye. Burt later
recalled that they turned eastward with relief, yet with many a backward
glance at "the grand mountains" that faded away behind them.[21]

Edward Berthoud and Silas Burt would never be so close again. Yet
their friendship was by no means at an end; twenty years later, Burt
had only the most flattering things to say of his old classmate.
Moreover, their recent investigations soon gave birth to a jointly
authored guidebook, *The Rocky Mountain Gold Regions,* probably the
best of a group of such publications, which Berthoud saw through the
Denver press of the *Rocky Mountain News.* It was a work of considerable
scope, embracing maps, statistics, and commentaries. The maps were
carefully executed, the statistics (especially as to mines and mills)
unique. The commentaries were mixed — an introductory historical
discussion was undistinguished, and the single paragraph about the
Indians was inadequate. The botanical essay that followed, however,

was positively erudite. Geographic and geologic matters were treated, by contemporary standards, with competence. Ultimately, there were two editions. On the title pages of both, Burt's name preceded Berthoud's; it was Ed's salute to a respected colleague.[22]

The departure of his associate did not leave Berthoud permanently despondent. Life in Golden City might lack certain amenities, but it was seldom tedious. He made new acquaintances, in particular William Austin Hamilton Loveland and George West. Loveland was of New England origin and Illinois seasoning; he had defied a youthful tendency to ill-health with unrestricted field service in the Mexican War, an overland trek to California, and a period of filibustering in Central America. He subsequently joined the rush to the Rockies not to seek gold, but to purvey the necessities to those who did, and therein he prospered. He presented a gangly appearance; his nose was prominent and his blue eyes keen. Now in his mid-thirties, he was about two years older than Berthoud.

George West had been one of Golden's pioneer "Boston Group" and had brought with him an extensive experience in journalism, especially on the prestigious *Boston Transcript*. In addition, he possessed a strong background of service in the Massachusetts militia. Though chiefly engaged in mercantile pursuits, he also printed an occasional newssheet called the *Western Mountaineer*. West had an irreverent sense of humor; some years later, when challenged to a duel, he chose as weapons "thundermugs at twenty paces, roll 'em or throw 'em." In 1860, he was about thirty years of age.[23]

Berthoud also kept in touch with his Leavenworth associates, especially Hugh and Tom Ewing, and before the end of 1860, their affiliation was suddenly rejuvenated by the rumored discovery, high among the headwaters of Clear Creek, a hitherto unnoticed breach in the mountain wall. Foothills gossip even suggested that it lay well below timberline. The Ewings had never abandoned their dream of a direct route, via "Pike's Peak," to Utah and the Pacific, and they at once urged Berthoud to organize, as soon as conditions permitted, a serious reconnaissance. Additional Kansans endorsed the proposal, while at the foot of the mountains, Golden City came quickly to fancy itself the key to the transcontinental commerce of North America. Only Denver demurred. Regional jealousies were already resolving themselves into a fundamental tension between the two little towns, and anything

Golden in the 1870s, a decade after the Berthouds settled there. *Courtesy of the Colorado Historical Society.*

that Berthoud might undertake obviously smacked of Golden.[24]

Yet, Denver did respect "progress," and on May 3, 1861, the *Rocky Mountain News* went so far as to encourage volunteers to join the survey party. The group was never, in fact, a large one; it totaled perhaps eight. Berthoud considered himself fortunate to acquire, at the last minute, the services of James Bridger, the renowned wilderness scout. The alleged pass was singularly elusive. It was then, and remains, quite invisible from either of its conventional approaches. Even Bridger was unaware of its existence, a professional deficiency that appears to have put him in a sour mood. He furthermore seems to have been instructed by a number of Kansans to search for more than one passage.[25]

The story of the first crossing of Berthoud Pass has been treated many times and need not be retold in detail. A base camp was established on May 10 beside the debris of a major avalanche; Bridger wandered sulkily off into an alternative valley, while Berthoud and most of the others pushed directly upward. It was their good fortune that the season was exceptionally mild. They encountered occasional melting snows, but had little need for snowshoes. As usual, the crest of the divide, permanently wind-swept, afforded open ground, and on May 12 Berthoud and his companions, moving easily along the skyline, literally tumbled into their pass. Several succeeding days were required to open a proper track, but on the 17th, complete with horses and mules, they negotiated most of the crossing. Berthoud later declared that it was accomplished "with surprising ease," but any veteran of the route may question this, and indeed his own formal report made explicit reference to snowbanks and deadfalls. They did tarry between flounderings to bestow their names upon prominent torrents and promontories. The pass itself was reserved for Berthoud.[26]

Beyond the divide lay the extensive intra-mountain opening called "Middle Park." It was already, in this unusual spring, well flowered, and the party rode briskly across it, skirting its uplifts. On May 21, an accidental grass fire produced consternation, but on the 22nd they encamped comfortably beside the Grand (Colorado) River in the midst of a scenic little basin. Just downstream, the river was sucked into the first of its celebrated canyons, and a major hot springs vented vapor. Westward, a straightforward ascent revealed open valleys and a gentle horizon.[27]

The men were jubilant. Before them, every prospect pleased, and

Looking south toward Berthoud Pass from near the present Mary Jane Ski Area. Photograph taken in the 1890s. *Courtesy of the Denver Public Library.*

they thereupon platted a city, engrossed ranches, and exchanged franchises. John K. Wright, in the role of secretary, drafted with imperfect literacy the by-laws of a "Middle Park Claim Club." Bridger, still confined within his alternative valley, was not included.[28]

By May 27 they were homeward bound. On Berthoud's pass the snow had almost totally disappeared. Berthoud himself rode on ahead astride a favorite mule, and by seven o'clock on the evening of the 28th was in Golden City. Two days later, the information he brought inspired a grand banquet and ball, an affair which lasted from noon to after midnight and was attended by numerous notables, including an official of the Overland Stage line, William H. Russell, the ex-governor of the now-defunct Territory of Jefferson, William Steele, and the constitutional governor of the newborn Territory of Colorado, William Gilpin. The dignitaries delivered speeches, and everyone partook of good cheer and great expectations.[29]

Nothing came of the Middle Park Claim Club; it expired quickly and without a struggle. But the transcontinental idea flourished; it was cordially supported by the Overland Stage Company of Bela M. Hughes, William H. Russell, and Ben Holladay, while back in Kansas the Ewings continued to be enthusiastic. Together they provided a sufficient subsidy to put Berthoud once again in the field at the head of a more elaborate expedition. It was ready to depart — from Denver — on July 6, 1861; its destination this time was Salt Lake City.[30]

Two members of the party, Thomas Moses and John K. Wright, had participated in the earlier reconnaissance, and Bridger, in a distinctly happier mood, was rehired as guide. Among the others were Berthoud's brothers-in-law, Frank and Charles Ferrell, and a highly competent young surveyor named Redwood Fisher. Following a routine traverse of Berthoud's pass, they were joined by the territorial Indian Agent, Harvey M. Vaile, together with a Dr. J. G. Edwards and three packers. Transportation was provided by nearly thirty horses and mules.[31]

It was, except for Bridger, a young group (Fisher was only 21); all were seasoned and robust. They traveled fast; westbound they attempted little more than an overview. It was not everywhere easy. The gentle horizon beyond Middle Park proved to be a mountain divide of respectable proportions. Bridger led them across it by an Indian trace that he had used in 1854 with the Anglo-Irish eccentric, Sir St. George Gore, and "Gore's Pass" was duly recorded in Berthoud's notes. They had now, in a geologic sense, completed their transit of the Rockies, but the plateaus ahead were still formidable, requiring repeated progressions between river valleys: from the Bear (Yampa) to the White (reached on July 21) and to the Green on July 25. They crossed the Green, which was 225 yards wide, on homemade rafts; their animals were induced to swim. Thereafter, they ascended the valleys of the Uintah River and its "De Chesne" fork to the watershed of the Great Basin. They entered Provo, via the Timpanogos Canyon, on the evening of August 1.[32]

After three weeks of wilderness travel, Berthoud thought Provo a "beautiful town." His remarks upon the journey itself were less precise. His route had taken him directly across a principal territory of the Ute Indians, yet he made no early reference to this. The expedition must, however, have encountered an Indian band or two, for Vaile in his own personal report worried openly over the effect of white men upon so "nicely adjusted a people." Berthoud did take note of the

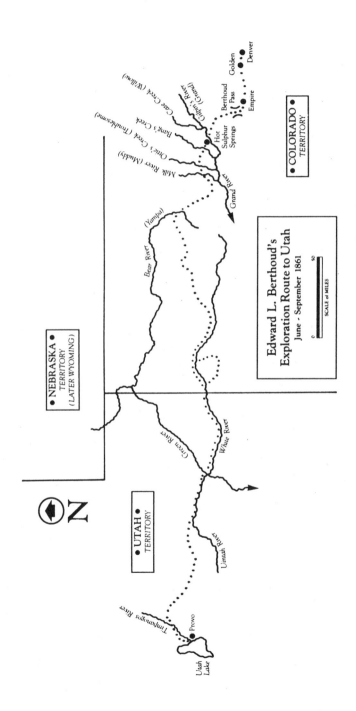

Edward L. Berthoud's
Exploration Route to Utah
June - September 1861

widely varied zones of vegetation, and he was delighted with the bird life, which beyond Gore Pass was extraordinarily tame. At their noon-day halts, cowbirds would light on the patched knee of his buckskins, and at the Green River the several species of ducks were quite fearless. On the Great Basin divide a "small sharp-shinned hawk" fairly adopted the party, perching successively on heads, firearms, and saddles. [33]

The party found the Utah settlements euphoric over the recent and hasty departure of the regional federal garrisons for service against the Southern Confederacy: Utah had been subjected to a kind of military occupation ever since the curious "Morman War" of 1857-8. "There is no constitutional government here," Berthoud reported, "and of course Gentiles will stand back." At Salt Lake City he sat, on Sunday, August 4, beneath the charismatic Elder Lorenzo Snow, who thundered a formal loyalty to the United States, yet openly stressed that the Saints should take advantage of this struggle of "Kilkenny Cats" to enhance their own interests. [34]

Harvey Vaile and two or three others chose to return by the regular South Pass stage, but Berthoud had been so encouraged by his direct transmountain route that he determined to establish it in detail. Fol-lowing a hurried refitting, his group selected as its datum the northeast corner of Brigham Young's Provo residence and, on August 10, de-parted. Existing surveys carried them upward into the scenic vale beneath the cirques of Mount Timpanogos, but thereafter all determi-nations were their own. [35]

The route differed little from their outward trek, but there were some probings (quickly abandoned) toward the headwaters of the White River and a cross-cut, using the Williams Fork of the Yampa, that avoided the northerly loop past Steamboat Springs. Chained distances, degrees of magnetic azimuth, and feet of vertical elevation were faith-fully and conventionally recorded, but Berthoud took additional pains to discover evidence of mineral deposits. He found considerable: gyp-sum and limestone abounded; there were suggestions of iron; and (most significant for the future) repeated signs of coal and "coal oil or naphtha." Indeed, Berthoud's were the first reports by a trained observer of the fabled energy resources of northwestern Colorado. He also attempted some landscape sketches of the Utah Book Cliffs and, in Colorado, of "Russell" (Toponas) Rock and the Rabbit Ears. They were without merit; Berthoud's inability to draw continued to be pronounced. They remain, however, the earliest representations of these well-known landforms that we have.[36]

Berthoud's party emerged from the Colorado foothills on September 17; the entire enterprise — men, animals, equipment, and subsistence — had cost its sponsors $3,000, which seemed, under the circumstances, a bargain. Berthoud's reports positively effervesced. The route, he pointed out, was remarkably short: from Provo to Denver it totaled 424⅜ miles, whereas by Bridger Pass in southern Wyoming it was 623 miles and by traditional South Pass, 841 miles. Consequently, it would shorten the distance from the Missouri River to California by at least 200 miles. It was generally less arid and afforded superior feed for stock. In certain areas it fairly sprouted telegraph poles. Berthoud reduced the considerable relief with encouraging words: a wagon road of "easy" grade could, he estimated, be put through for no more than $400,000. He even took time to expound (contrary to habit) upon the superior beauty of the scenery.[37]

Any resident of northwestern Colorado will at once perceive the grand deficiency — nothing was said about winter. Berthoud himself could not have been unaware of this inconvenience, but he apparently fell into the common error of subsidized explorers in trying too hard to please his patrons. Even so, he let slip a reservation or two. From the first he insisted that any railroad would require a two-mile tunnel beneath the continental divide; moreover, toward the end of the journey, he privately admitted to being weary of sagebrush. Jim Bridger never offered a formal endorsement, and his well-known personal illiteracy may not have been the only reason. Several months later, the realistic Redwood Fisher could no longer contain himself, and in a public letter, scarcely concealed beneath a *nom-de-plume*, he bluntly charged Berthoud with unwarranted optimism.[38]

Nevertheless, most Coloradoans preferred to be optimistic. On October 18, 1861, the new territorial legislature incorporated a wagon road company which proposed an early extension westward over Berthoud's Pass, and indeed this enterprise became the corporate ancestor of the first railroad to penetrate the Colorado mountains. On November 6, there appeared a "Colorado and Pacific Wagon, Telegraph and Railroad Company," which specified Berthoud's route in every detail. In any case, his survey figures were commendably accurate, and the maps that were derived from them proved useful for many years.[39]

Most important of all, the Berthoud investigations of 1861 served to ripen a dream, the vision of Leavenworth and the Ewings, of a Colorado astride the central main line of North America. It was from the beginning a questionable notion and was condemned to long frustration, and even its latter-day fulfillment still carries serious qualificatoins — the high Rockies continue to have their say.

But of a suitable name for Berthoud Pass, there has never been any question.

CHAPTER III

War as a Bore;
Peace as Frustration

On May 12, 1861, when Ed Berthoud and his companions stood for the first time upon the summit of his pass, the American Civil War was precisely one month old. That they were aware of this may be doubted; any special concern for their country's future must have been eclipsed by the satisfaction of the moment. Moreover, as residents of the infant Territory of Colorado they were separated from the crisis by the equivalent of an ocean, and indeed "the Plains" have remained a basic and mystical concept for Coloradoans to this day. Furthermore, the national disruption was still widely perceived as provisional, and its principal early effect in Colorado was a reemphasis upon the central rather than the southern transcontinental stage route, a consequence that helped send Berthoud off upon his second expedition on July 6.[1]

But on July 21, just as his party was threading the dusty tablelands toward the White River, the memorable battle at Bull Run, Virginia, changed everything. Thereafter, it was clear that the reduction of the Southern Confederacy would be long, harsh, and not necessarily successful.[2]

Nor was this all. During the weeks of Berthoud's return from Utah, rebel forces were winning unexpected victories in western Missouri, and for a time it appeared that Colorado (chiefly Unionist in outlook) would be denied the use of its principal line of communication with the east.[3]

The difficulties multiplied. Few of the original "Pike's Peak" mines had generated instant wealth; most had been established in innocence;

others would require the kind of investment in money and equipment that was now unavailable. There was a pause in the excitement; it was, in truth, a depression, and it swiftly reduced the demand for Berthoud's professional services. The Confederate threat continued. The South was dreaming imperial dreams — of a corridor to the Pacific and a war effort backed with gold. Throughout the fall and winter of 1861-62, alarming reports drifted up from New Mexico. The whole southern half of that territory had fallen into rebel hands, and in February a considerable array of Texans began an advance up the Rio Grande toward Santa Fe and the Rocky Mountain mining settlements. 4

Stagnation within and danger without now produced a sudden martial flurry. It was deficient in resources and not perfectly attuned to accepted financial practices, but it swept Berthoud into the Union army on March 23, 1862. Whether his motives were economic or patriotic is not perfectly clear; most likely, he simply followed the lead of his friend, George West, who had found it expedient to abandon a faltering newspaper in order to recruit and command a company of volunteers. 5

West's Company H was based in Golden; its regiment was the Second Colorado Volunteer Infantry. West, with his background in the Massachusetts militia, made a competent captain, but the regiment, an array of pedestrians in a land of uncompromising distances, quickly acquired a reputation for infinite drudgery, unspiced by the presence of Confederates. Berthoud, as a first lieutenant, had frequent access to a saddle, but this simply expanded the perimeters of a dreary service; in addition, his obviously superior education repeatedly condemned him to the routines of administrative duty. It is among the logistics of the conflict that we discover the essence of Edward Berthoud's Civil War.

His first responsibilities were as a recruiter, in Golden and in the upper mining camps. For two months he sat in flapping tents, dispatching volunteers to an inchoate mustering place called Camp Weld, which was named for the territorial secretary and which lay across the South Platte River from Denver. One of the enlistees was Berthoud's twenty-one-year-old brother-in-law, Frank Ferrell. Berthoud's authority was imperfect; for weeks he acted by private suggestions from George West, and his "appointment" by the regimental commander, Colonel Jesse H. Leavenworth, was not forthcoming until May 14. Even then his status was provisional, pending confirmation through uncertain channels from the east.[6]

Early in June, the Second Colorado was pronounced ready for field service. The Territory by this time felt relatively secure. The Missouri situation had improved, and in the course of the spring an emergency contingent of "Pike's Peakers" had at Glorieta Pass, New Mexico, thrust the Texans back upon El Paso. There lingered, however, much official concern for the safety of the Santa Fe Trail. This long-established route spanned a quarter-continent of open space, perilously close to Confederate horizons, and all serious traffic had in consequence been diverted to its northwestern, or "mountain" division. But even this segment was deemed exposed, and the military ultimately decided upon an elaborate program of garrison and escort between Fort Larned, Kansas, and Raton Pass, at the New Mexico border, a distance of nearly 400 miles. To this awkward duty the Second Colorado was now committed.[7]

The men were sent forward piecemeal. Most were initially concentrated at Fort Lyon, an existing post on the Arkansas River about forty-five miles west of the Kansas line. For some reason, possibly under-recruitment, Captain West's Company H did not move until autumn, but Berthoud himself was ordered out upon a variety of assignments. Most involved arduous travel. The first entailed the transfer of the regimental artillery — a single battery — from Camp Weld to Fort Lyon. The unit was not of Colorado origin. The gunners had recently arrived from Wisconsin, while their field pieces were antiques, captured from the Confederates. Berthoud accompanied the movement as regimental liaison officer, but in fact was in effective command. The route was classic: up the valley of Cherry Creek, across the high "Pineries," past Pikes Peak at its grandest, and thence south and east into the Arkansas Valley. Henri Chatillon had conducted Francis Parkman this way sixteen summers before.[8]

They departed Camp Weld on June 23 in exceptional heat; later they marched through thunder and rain, and on the evening of the 29th they camped for the night near the site of Olney Springs. This represented excellent time, but their final stint was prodigious. Skirting the dissolving rubble of Old Bent's Fort, they pressed eastward almost without pause to Fort Lyon itself, arriving at 9:30 on the morning of July 1. They had traveled, on and off caissons, some 66 miles. Even

Captain Berthoud of Company F, Second Colorado Cavalry, seen here in less formal field dress. Although Berthoud saw little action, the strain of war seems apparent. *Courtesy of the Colorado Historical Society.*

Berthoud admitted to excessive fatigue.[9]

Fort Lyon, lately Fort Wise and originally "New Bent's Fort," presented an assortment of stone buildings and corrals, sited (very imprudently) upon the flood plain of the Arkansas; atop an adjacent terrace, the original Bent premises perched safe, sound, and largely unused. Tents, personnel, and picket lines littered the area; close at hand a minor tributary disgorged sand.[10]

Here the greater part of the Second Colorado and, in theory, Lieutenant Berthoud, would be stationed for more than twelve months. But Berthoud was at once sent out upon additional tasks: direct passages over the plains to Denver, a wagon journey of 300 miles along the mountain front to Fort Union, New Mexico, and detached activities down the Arkansas, deep into Kansas. The Denver expeditions were intended to develop shorter lines of communication from Camp Weld to Fort Lyon; the New Mexico visit (so brief that Berthoud's name does not appear on the surviving records of Fort Union) was concerned with the "repatriation" of certain Coloradoans who had become entangled in New Mexico units; the probes into Kansas did not fully develop until the following spring.[11]

Little is known of these episodes. Many years later Berthoud declared that the return from New Mexico had involved an exhausting solo ride from the Raton Pass to Fort Lyon (about 130 miles) in just two days and that his rations enroute had consisted of one chunk of ham and a half-loaf of hard bread. "But," he recalled, "my teeth were good [and] as a French wit said, 'Nous avons changé tout cela'. (We've changed all that.)"[12]

At the beginning of August, he was ordered back to Denver upon a second tour of recruiting; it must have been a pressing need, for he was allowed the assistance of a sergeant, a musician, and a private.[13] Nevertheless, he did find time to consult privately with Peter A. Dey, a reconnaissance engineer for the embryo Union Pacific Railway.[14]

There was also a family crisis. His mother-in-law had been in delicate health for nearly a year, and in September John Ferrell took Jeannette east for treatment. It was in vain; late in October they reached the home of a cousin at Portage, New York, where on November 2 she died. Whether Helen Berthoud accompanied them is unknown, but Mr. Ferrell quickly disposed of most of his Golden properties and settled for good in upstate New York.[15]

Berthoud remained on duty in the Denver area through the remainder of the year; after the recruiting came the erection of cavalry stables
at Camp Weld. In mid-September a much-traveled military pouch
brought — at last — his formal commission as first lieutenant. He
was to rank not from his March 23 arrangement with Captain West,
but his May 14 appointment by Colonel Leavenworth.[16]

This "home service" came officially to an end in January 1863, and
by February he was back at Fort Lyon. He by now was fully committed
to the Santa Fe road. Early in April he was appointed regimental
adjutant and a few weeks later assistant adjutant general "of all the
troops on this route," a duty concerned with the placement of units
and their equipment. He was again frequently in the saddle, enduring
punishing rides beneath blazing skies. No Confederates appeared.[17]

Berthoud's headquarters were presently moved to Fort Larned, a
conglomerate of slab and sod deep in central Kansas, where the western
meadowlark and the (eastern) cardinal sometimes sang together. He
may have noted this with interest. But it was as tedious an assignment
as a subaltern could face. Between trail missions he counted blankets
and wagon-tongues and suffered the lamentations of Colonel Leavenworth, who yearned for a more positive glory. "There is," growled the
Colonel, "no more necessity for troops in this place than at Syracuse,
N.Y."[18]

Berthoud did enjoy a respite, a late-June diversion to the edge of
the real war, down the long ruts to the woodland fringes and on to
district headquarters in Kansas City. There he delivered dispatches
and tarried briefly with his old associate, Thomas Ewing, who now
wore the stars of a brigadier general. But Berthoud saw no combat and
quickly returned to Fort Larned through massive heat, bearing orders
and endorsements. (Those acquainted with the *minutiae* of the war
will note that he had nicely evaded the horrors of Quantrill's Raid
and of Ewing's bitter response which placed the entire Missouri border
under martial law.)[19]

Fort Larned continued humdrum. A considerable contingent of the
Second Colorado, including Golden's Company H, was ordered east;
under the stern pressures of the plains they had become, unofficially,
a mounted infantry, and they soon experienced successful combat
along the frontiers of Arkansas. Upon the trail behind them they left
tatters of units, bored and unkempt. At Fort Larned, Jesse Leaven-

worth's frustrations became aberrations, and when in July clusters of migrant Indians appeared on the skyline he reported by express rider that his post was surrounded by pro-Confederate tribesmen. But the Colonel's battle-wish went unfulfilled, and Berthoud passed the remainder of the summer performing administrative chores and routine treks. He bore them all without complaint. He remained an essential engineer, a proud profession indeed, but typically subject to the directives of others. Subordination came easily — more easily perhaps than leadership.[20]

There would be no break in the tedium until October, when higher authorities in St. Louis announced the merging of the Second Colorado Infantry into a reconstituted and completely re-equipped Second Colorado Cavalry. Additional orders assigned Berthoud to a new Company E, but a supplementary paragraph placed him, as usual, on detached duty, this time as assistant adjutant general under General Ewing. Obviously, he had been spoken for.[21]

Alas, Berthoud could not leave Fort Larned until December 1; the red-tape of the wagon tongues forbade it. When at last he did go, his progress was dramatic, and on the evening of the 4th he was signing the primitive register at the Union Hotel in Kansas City. By this time he had developed the endurance of a Cheyenne warrior, but a ride of this nature (280 miles through exceptionally foul weather) surpasses belief. Perhaps he secured a place on the mail stage.[22]

Berthoud enjoyed his stint with Ewing, but it lasted no more than a month. Shortly after the New Year (1864) he was swept on to St. Louis to participate in the formal muster of the Second Colorado Cavalry. This was hardly necessary; he was cited as First Lieutenant of Company E, but with the understanding that his adjutant's tour would continue, and he was back in Kansas City (following a journey by rail and by mud) on January 23. There he found himself under a new superior officer, Colonel James Hobart Ford, who not only commanded the new Second Colorado, but also had assumed authority — in place of Ewing — over the Fourth Sub-District of the District of Central Missouri.[23]

Berthoud was often fortunate in his military superiors. He had liked Ewing, and he at once liked Ford. This unusual man had entered the army with the credentials of a wholesale druggist, yet quickly had demonstrated the instincts of a born field commander. Twenty years later, Berthoud remembered him with unfeigned admiration. The good feelings were mutual; Ford himself soon came to trust Berthoud explicitly. [24]

Berthoud was fortunate in another respect. Fate continued its habit of sparing him from the hazards of combat. This was curious as his adjutant's office (at the "House of L. Carter") stood conspicuously on a river bluff and squarely in the midst of the most unpleasant theater of the war. Guerrilla activities, both Union and Confederate, were desolating the entire Missouri border and had even penetrated the outskirts of Kansas City itself; moreover, with spring the butchery intensified, and Berthoud found himself in a clearing house for horror. Dispatch bearers, frequently blood-smeared, delivered appalling reports, which it was his principal duty to assemble and transmit to St. Louis. He also was responsible for casualty lists and for the pitiful personal effects of the slain. He also scrutinized the activities of the local citizenry, and sometimes, in the absences of Colonel Ford, found himself conducting campaigns of counter-insurgency from his desk. Yet for months he never sniffed gunpowder, and his principal personal crisis involved a reception and ball, given by his colleagues in honor of two visiting actresses. [25]

This strange interlude finally came to an end in June 1864, when the next higher military echelon, the District of Central Missouri, discovered a need for a topographical engineer. Administrative procedures, one of which required a rectification of Berthoud's personal inititials on his orders, occupied the greater part of a month, but at the beginning of July he departed for Warrensburg, Missouri, to assume his new duties. With him went a gaggle of casuals; they were a singularly helpless group, yet attracted no snipers. They were home free in Warrensburg by the afternoon of the 3rd. [26]

Warrensburg was as pleasant a situation as a distracted Missouri could offer. It perched dapple-shaded upon the swell of a little plateau; at its fringes an array of tents and hasty out-buildings bore the name of Camp Grover, in honor of a slain local hero of Unionist sympathies. District headquarters had been established in the local courthouse, a compact little structure of distinctive architectural merit. Berthoud's new commander was General Egbert Benson Brown, bluff, balding and forty-eight, no West Pointer, but with a solid background in a variety of military situations, pitched battles included. Of greatest consequence, however, was the nearby railhead of the Pacific Railroad of Missouri, a long-stagnant enterprise that military necessity had lately revived. Its line was now being extended toward Kansas City upon a spacious gauge of five feet six inches.[27]

Berthoud concentrated upon the railroad. Eastward from Warrensburg its track was half-derelict; westward, gangs of loosely disciplined graders picked and shoveled upon its slowly advancing right of way. Over everything hung the threat of guerrilla assault, and the majority of Berthoud's activities were concerned with emergency defenses. Yet his role as a uniformed non-combatant continued, and he experienced little if any hostile gunfire. Early in August he was promoted to captain (technically of the Second Cavalry's Company D, but again on detached duty), and almost simultaneously he was joined by his wife.[28]

His promotion was routine; the sole blot upon his existing record was the loss of "one tin spittoon." But the appearance of Helen requires explanation. Whence she came is uncertain, but we do know that her arrival at this half-beleagured headquarters occasioned no comment. The American Civil War, in particular its western theaters, positively welcomed the presence of women — wives or otherwise. In fact, women were accorded quasi-official status; the consorts of officers were received as "nurses," those of enlisted men as "washerwomen." In an environment of cornfield sniping and camp epidemics the nurses were more than decorative, and every surviving reference certifies to Helen Berthoud's remarkable aptitude for the healing arts. She furthermore was never in particular danger, for the curious folkways of the "border" held women (though not always their property) sacrosanct.[29]

She even found time for her husband. Through August and most of September they boarded together (at $5.50 per week, each) with a succession of Warrensburg families, and we learn that upon one occasion they took part in an "assembly of fair women and brave men" that danced a summer's night away at the little courthouse. But Warrensburg's immunities were more apparent than real, and they were brutally disrupted late in September by General Sterling Price's final effort to win Missouri for the Confederacy. By the 24th the entire District headquarters — personnel, records, and furnishings — was fleeing toward Sedalia aboard a special train, and on October 1 Captain Berthoud found himself directing the construction of emergency earth-

The Johnson County Courthouse, Warrensburg, Missouri, the center of Berthoud's military in the summer of 1864. *Courtesy of Robert C. Black, III.*

works about the perimeter of Jefferson City. Under him labored "100 negroes and 1500 men" [*sic!*], together with an unspecified number of inmates from the state penitentiary; behind him in the town an ill-assorted garrison of perhaps 6,000 stood nervously to arms. The oncoming Confederates were rumored to number 20,000. [30]

The test came on October 7. Picket firing sounded from the southeast, and presently the long, ragged files of Price's Southerners emerged from the nearby woods; some deployed into line of battle; others sited field guns. Orders were passed by voice and gesture, and abruptly the rebel guns burst into flickers of flame and puffs of sulphurous smoke. The Union artillery (no more than eight pieces) banged in reply, while the infantry in Berthoud's rifle pits thudded out volleys. The air was shredded by hostile projectiles, and a few of the defenders sank into the earth, but many more of the Confederates were knocked down, never to rise again. Once or twice a glitter of steel suggested a charge, but it never came, either on that day or on the following morning, when the firing gradually slackened and the enemy retired westward, away from Jefferson City.[31]

It had been, so far as the records indicate, Edward Berthoud's only taste of battle. It also could be cited as his particular victory. General Price had recoiled from his fortifications. Berthoud even received honorable mention in dispatches. The experience rather whetted his spirits; this is clear from his field notes, which he preserved, and it is likely that he hankered for more. But it was not to be. On the 14th he was directed to join the staff of the departmental commander, Major General William Starke Rosecrans, an officer lofty in rank and notable in administration, but given to conducting his operations (as per the manual) from the rear. Berthoud was of necessity condemned to a traverse of recent battlegrounds, past the litter of the lately engaged, through Sedalia, Lexington, Independence, and Westport, then south along the ruler's edge of Kansas. There, close to the fringes of Arkansas, the Confederates disintegrated. Berthoud remained throughout underutilized and unmentioned, and we can only imagine his reaction when he heard the francophone *Marais des Cygnes* (river and battlefield) referred to locally as "Mary Dayson!"[32]

Thereafter his prospects seemed to improve. The Pacific Railroad had been severely mauled, and he was reassigned, once more at Warrensburg, to its restoration. However, Price's collapse had so dispirited the regional guerrillas that the Second Colorado was presently judged to be superfluous in Missouri, and when repeated border rumors suggested that a final Confederate effort, spiced with Indians, might be expected on the open plains, Colonel Ford was directed to move every available unit, the Coloradoans in particular, into Kansas to meet it. The transfer was brisk; the final elements, Captain and Mrs. Berthoud included, rode into Fort Riley during Christmas week. According to Berthoud's personal orders, he was at last intended for company command.[33]

This, once more, was not to be. He did assume formal responsibility for Company D and retained it, technically, until the end, but most of his unit was quickly removed from his control and distributed piecemeal across the western spaces. He even lost his principal subaltern, a balding, competent little German named Billy Wise, to scouting operations out of Council Grove, and with Wise went a cadre of his most experienced men. It was probably inevitable that Colonel Ford

Colonel James A. Ford, Berthoud's principal commander, in Kansas City in 1864. *Courtesy of the Denver Public Library.*

should recall him to staff duty, and on April 29, 1865, he was invested with the office of district inspector general. It was the old story — dull administration, dull logistics, and, as chance would have it, an honorable escape from combat.[34]

The winter was pleasant enough. Fort Riley occupied a noble site and, barring troublesome chimney flues, afforded superior facilities. There was an array of amenities — better washing, better bathing, and, on March 3, 1865, a presidential ball beneath garlands and crossed sabres. Even the weather was benign; for weeks it suggested early spring. But beyond the horizon the Confederate war continued, nor was it wholly over when, on April 10, the telegraph brought confirmation of Lee's surrender. Moreover, as the Southern danger waned, the aboriginal waxed. For a variety of reasons, in particular the tragic slaughter on November 29, 1864, at Sand Creek, Colorado, the plains tribes were in a sullen mood.[35]

General Ford proposed to cope with them by posting his elements (chiefly cavalry) along, or close to, the Santa Fe Trail, in convenient array for concentration. This was the reason for the dividing and subdividing of Berthoud's company, and it eventually committed Berthoud to renewed mounted duty. From April onward we find him repeatedly at Fort Larned and at the newly established outposts named Zarah and Ellsworth. No hostiles appeared, but once among the cottonwoods by Fort Ellsworth he noted a flock of his beloved parakeets.[36]

Ford's program would eventually be frustrated, not by Indians, but by the Indian Bureau. Resident Kansans, long savaged by guerrillas, were in no mood for further distresses, and their peace-yearnings found an unlikely champion in Jesse H. Leavenworth, the frustrated fire-eater of 1863. For want of glory, Leavenworth had resigned his military commission, but now, as United States Indian Agent for the Upper Arkansas, he assumed a dove's plumage. His influence, and the appeals of Kansas congressmen, produced such confusing orders that the combat-eager Ford rode, in his turn, to Fort Leavenworth and turned in his sabre. He was replaced on July 1 by Brevet Major General J.B. Sanborn, who, in the fashion of the highly ranked, brought along his own inspector general. Berthoud was thereupon kicked sideways into the role of "district engineer," which was suitable in theory but a fiction in fact. His duties continued as before — rigorous trail errands and, at Fort Riley, the paper administration of Company D. In pursuit of the latter he sat upon petty military courts, assessed the battle-worthiness of halters, and sought the return of sundry saddles that had disappeared down the Kansas River in a skiff. At one point it was even suggested that he should build a bridge across the mouth of the Republican River.[37]

He would he held to this treadmill to the end. Occasional gunfire sounded across the Kansas spaces, and one of Berthoud's best noncommissioned officers was pursued, slaughtered, and desecrated at Running Turkey Creek, less than seventy miles west of Council Grove. A major chapter of plains warfare was in fact in the offing, yet it did not really seem so that summer, and the tedium of the service overcame even Berthoud's good nature. Worse still, a sequence of errors, to which even the best ordered military administration is occasionally subject, had denied him his salary since the end of January. This meant months of awkward penury and an embarrassing limitation upon the social activities expected of an officer and his lady.[38]

It was mid-September of 1865 before he was able to proceed to Fort Leavenworth, where on the 23rd he was mustered out of the military. He did receive his final pay, but $4.29 was carefully deducted, thanks to the disappearance of one cap-pouch, two bullet moulds, and 160 company badges.[39]

Over the three and one-half years of his service he had never become a conspicuous leader, save possibly at Jefferson City; yet he had always been useful, especially in the performance of the kinds of drudgery without which no army can remain effective for very long.

Nor was it a service without heroism. The "border" theater of the American Civil War was beyond doubt the most terrible of them all, and everyone in uniform who found himself on duty there faced the possibility, even the likelihood, of sudden death. Berthoud, though under serious fire but once, had been nonetheless in mortal danger over many uninterrupted months.

*   *   *

The demobilization of the Second Colorado sent many of its veterans straightway back to the territory; indeed, a considerable number risked the direct plains crossing by way of the Smoky Hill. But Ed and Helen hesitated. Perhaps to their surprise, they had come to feel rather at home in the service, and though they did turn presently westward, it was by stages along the conventional Platte route and as civilian adjuncts of the military. Berthoud in essence simply continued, as a private citizen, many of his previous duties.[40]

More specifically, he secured a position as a chief quartermaster's clerk, charged with the supply of the Seventh Iowa Volunteer Cavalry, a conglomeration of wartime residuals, not necessarily from Iowa, that had been given the task of protecting the Platte River emigrant routes. Berthoud was first allotted a primitive office at Fort Cottonwood (later McPherson), twelve miles to the east of the forks of the Platte. Later, beginning in December 1865, he was stationed at Fort Sedgwick, an uncouth quadrilateral of frame and sod close to the northeastern corner of Colorado. But much of his time was spent on the road, inspecting wayside outposts — Alkali, Nebraska, was one — and drawing upon the regional depots at Fort Kearney and Denver. His salary was $150.00 per month. His status was civilian, but he remained socially within the officer caste, and everyone continued to address him as "captain." The title would never leave him; former military rank was a particular and cherished perquisite of his generation.[41]

The Berthouds were neither very lonely nor very bored. The trail traffic was constant; visitors, official or casual, were frequent, and more than one took special note of Helen's graciousness. Moreover, the captain found time to subdivide (provisionally) a nearby tract of semi-desert; he called it Julesburg after the well-known but recently incinerated Overland Stage station. Julesburg restored would one day become a credit to the "verdant Platte," he declared. Meanwhile it could serve as a distribution point for a popular Great Plains benefaction known as "rifle whiskey." On his visits to Denver he often paused for gossip at the hospitable new saloon of his former first lieutenant, Billy Wise, and he sometimes continued to Golden to dabble further in land (the latter activity produced, on paper, an extensive dream property called, for obscure reasons, "Lunatic Monster Ranch"). As with his pre-war speculations it was all more whimsical than real, and the same could be said of his drinking.[42]

By the spring of 1866 it was clear that Ed Berthoud would not spend the rest of his life with the army. He initiated a regular correspondence with friends in Golden; for "Ozello" (a newspaper correspondent) he identified a semi-aquatic songbird as the water ouzel, and for the innovative William A.H. Loveland he drew up an elaborate commentary on mountain railroads. The latter would prove significant. Somewhere among his professional papers the captain had come upon several notices of the Festiniog Railway, a Welsh enterprise in difficult terrain that had been built on a gauge of one foot, eleven-and-one-half inches. (It also had become, as of 1863, the first steam-powered, narrow gauge common carrier in the world.) Berthoud thought the narrow gauge a promising concept for Colorado, because such a line would require far less grading and would permit much lighter rolling stock. He went further. For the crossing of the continental divide, and perhaps for the penetration of the more precipitous canyons, he suggested a system of stationary engines and inclined planes, similar in pattern to those on the Morris Canal in New Jersey. The latter notion was of course radical, possibly absurd, and no one, except occasionally Berthoud, took it at all seriously. But the narrow gauge idea caught on and would presently transform the face of the Rocky Mountain West.[43]

Ed and Helen left Fort Sedgwick and the army on July 4, 1866; they reached Denver on the 13th and proceeded at once to Golden. Their commitment to the place was already firm, and they quickly re-established themselves in their sparse little "Miner's House." Although Golden still had a barren look (and would continue so for decades), its amenities were probably superior to those of a military outpost. Golden also offered "prospects." Berthoud promptly acquired, for one dollar, seven additional vacant lots, following which he published a carefully crafted estimate of the city's future growth. But he was most intrigued with the talk of "Bill" Loveland, whom he found deep in plans for a railroad. It was not as yet the mountain narrow gauge, but a more spacious concept, the routing of the first American transcontinental, standard gauge and all, directly across the spine of Colorado. Golden, naturally, would become a foot-of-the-mountains division point. Loveland, in fact, was ready with an incorporation called the Colorado Central & Pacific, on the board of which he had contrived to place five representatives of the still-nascent Union Pacific.[44]

The Union Pacific had by now a starting place, Council Bluffs, Iowa, and a width of four feet, eight-and-one-half inches, both established by law, but its route across the continental divide was as yet undetermined. This posed a dilemma: should the company select moderate mountains and no population — southern Wyoming — or serious

The Berthouds' home in Golden at 714 11th Street, as it looked in the 1930s. *Courtesy of the Colorado Historical Society.*

mountains and established settlements — Colorado? Loveland cordially suggested the latter and offered, largely at his own expense, a detailed feasibility study. He also presented as a kind of package Captain Berthoud and his pass.[45]

That a railroad would differ from a stage road Berthoud understood as well as anyone, and he was fully aware that Congress had prescribed for the new transcontinental a maximum gradient of 2 ¼ percent. His knowledge of the terrain was of course unexcelled, and the Union Pacific accepted his collaboration with alacrity. The study began briskly. Berthoud established a provisional line through Clear Creek Canyon in a matter of days, and before the end of August he had determined that its South Fork passes would be too awkward for a standard gauge. His old route promised better, and an auspicious reconnaissance was run through it and into Middle Park during the month of September. Much of the field work was performed by the captain himself; his principal colleague was Percy T. Browne of the Union

Pacific, a young engineer of great promise, but with tragedy in his future. (He was killed by Indians in southern Wyoming.) Confident in the expectation of federal subsidies, they resorted, while in the canyon, to nearly a mile of tunneling and on the divide to a bore of two-and-three-quarter miles beneath the pass itself. These, they found, would yield a grade within the maximum. [46]

The Union Pacific was clearly encouraged, and in mid-September the Browne-Berthoud party was joined by the company's famous chief engineer, General Grenville M. Dodge, two consulting engineers, Messrs. Seymour and Cheeseborough, and the government representative on the Union Pacific board, Jesse L. Williams. Together they re-examined Berthoud Pass and pronounced it good. There followed much backslapping in Denver and Golden, but then came discomfiture. The expedition turned its attention to alternative routes, and on November 7, as they contemplated the site of the later crossing at Rollins Pass, winter struck. Wind and snow beyond imagination swept them from the tundra lip and into the high cirques of Middle Boulder Creek; in a blinding whiteout they cut their animals loose, listened to their faint and fatal crashings, and scarcely reached the shelter of the timber themselves. [47]

For the Union Pacific representatives it was enough. They made no effort to discover whether conditions on Berthoud's pass might have been less terrible, and from the foothills General Dodge summarily canceled Colorado by telegraph. The government director, Williams, completed the rejection at length and in writing in March 1867. [48]

The Union Pacific debacle was, of course, a sharp disappointment. But the fates were by no means through with Berthoud that season. Hardly had he brushed off the snows of Rollins Pass when he was forced to undergo a public humiliation of the most unpleasant kind. It had a political basis. 1866 had been an election year for the territorial legislature, and Berthoud had returned from the army precisely at the beginning of the canvass. The "Unionist" (Radical) Republicans of Jefferson County promptly experienced a brainstorm. Here was "availability" in faded uniform. Here was "education" with an eastern degree and five foreign languages. Here was a "professional" in a discipline greatly sought after in a pioneer community. Here was even "popularity" — slight charisma, perhaps, but no one, literally, no one, disliked him. A spontaneous call was swiftly arranged, and on August 7 the

The Loveland Building in Golden, where the legislature met when Berthoud served as speaker of the Territorial House. *Courtesy of Robert C. Black, III.*

captain was elected the member for "Vasquez" District (Clear Creek) in the Territorial House of Representatives on the Radical Republican ticket. The returns were a miniature landslide — 1888 to 98. His delighted sponsors chose to ignore his political past and talents.[49]

The territorial capital had not yet been permanently established in Denver, and the new legislature gathered on December 3 in Golden; the lower house, Berthoud included, occupied a bare little hall in the Loveland Block on Washington Street. Tension pervaded the tobacco haze; it was intra, rather than inter, party in character, and the quarrels that counted involved principally those who called themselves "Republican." Each faction, radical or moderate, nursed opposite notions as to possible statehood, Indian policy, and the current territorial governor, and each had its favorite candidate for congressional delegate. Moreover, whenever the Republican moderates chose to act in conjunction with the minority Democrats, the House found itself in perfect — and distinctly awkward — equilibrium. But many of the Republican radicals continued to fancy Berthoud as a malleable catspaw, and on the first day of the session, amid extensive log-rolling, he was elected Speaker of the House of Representatives by a vote of 12 to 11.[50]

There was immediate trouble. The two Republican factions clashed bitterly over credentials, an issue which would determine the choice of territorial delegate. Berthoud, in the chair, violated no specific rule of order, but his preference for the moderates became quickly apparent. The radicals were furious; they were restrained during formal sessions by the rules of the House, but vituperation burst from their newspapers in a noxious cloud. "Villain," shrieked the *Rocky Mountain News,* "renegade," "dotard," "addle brain," "deserter from the side of liberty and Union;" "Captain, your present voyage will end in Davy Jones' locker, in a sea of political oblivion." The Central City *Register* was as bad. It accused Berthoud of selling his honor for the speakership and pronounced him "weak minded," "naturally worthless," and a "renegade of the first water." Seldom has an American office holder been so grievously abused, and it is a revealing comment upon Edward L. Berthoud that he endured it with scarcely a murmur; in fact, on New Year's Day he and Helen entertained the entire legislature "at a table groaning under an abundance of good things," and his sole personal retort was a mildly off-color reference to the *Rocky Mountain News* several months later. He of course did not suffer in solitude; the Republican moderates and Democrats clasped him to their bosoms, while his friend and fellow veteran, George West, sprang to his defense in a brand-new Democratic paper, published in Golden, called the *Colorado Transcript.* Moreover, the House itself, at its January adjournment, adopted unanimously a resolution commending the Speaker for the "able and efficient and impartial manner" in which he had presided.[51]

It is probably fair to say that Berthoud, as speaker, favored positions and policies that he deemed good for the community, regardless of party considerations, and in truth his behavior in the chair smacked of the parliamentary rather than the congressional. The basic difficulty lay in the fact that his radical Republican sponsors had neglected to ascertain what his opinions were and that he was, in his quiet way, really a Democrat. The session, in consequence, appeared to many to have been unproductive. There was no progress toward statehood; efforts to embarrass the governor, the controversial and widely unpopular Alexander Cummings, got nowhere; and a territorial militia bill, necessary to secure a federal subsidy, was not acted upon at all. Only one really popular measure, designed to keep blacks off juries, was adopted — over the governor's veto and Berthoud's private advice.[52]

In the final analysis, however, the *Rocky Mountain News* was right. When the session ended, Berthoud entered the political wilderness. It was partly his own choice; never again would he seek major office. Yet, he could never sustain a complete divorce from public concerns. His education and background forbade it. His profession itself was often of a semi-official character, and his remarkable avocations carried him constantly into print and onto the lecture platform. Nor did he eschew lesser public roles. Between January 1867 and November 1869, he acted occasionally as deputy territorial treasurer. During much of 1867, he served as territorial librarian and, from 1868 to 1871, as Jefferson County Commissioner. He even became a delegate to the Territorial Democratic Convention in June 1868. His performance as treasurer was mixed: there were deficiencies in the Military Poll and in the Miners' Relief and Poor funds, and he resigned his post slightly in debt to the territory. At the convention he was comfortable as a professing Democrat, but avoided serious leadership. His stint in the library, though brief, was happy; he developed a small collection of surprising quality and, except for his numerous field trips, attended faithfully to his duties. He supervised a detailed statistical review of Jefferson County. He was, as usual, most completely at home with natural history and to the Smithsonian Institution he contributed data upon local weather and Indian antiquities. He corresponded at length with the respected geologist, Professor James D. Dana, concerning "Aezoic" (Precambrian) rocks. His weather chart contained erroneous figures as to altitude, and his conclusions upon the rocks have long since been superceded, but he so impressed contemporary scholars that before the end of 1867 he was elected a corresponding member of the Philadelphia Academy of Arts and Sciences and of the Lyceum of Natural History at New York.[53]

There also were private activities. The records of Jefferson County are filled with his real estate transactions. He launched, in association with a young Denver insurance man named George E. Crater, an agency in Golden for life, fire and accident. Through his Union College classmate, Frederick W. Seward, he sought an arrangement with the

The Golden House, Calvary Church, and the South Side School (under construction) in 1873. At this time Golden still dreamed of outstripping Denver. *Courtesy of the Denver Public Library.*

U.S. Department of State — for what purpose is no longer clear. Seward's response was faintly top-lofty: "I am glad to hear of you again and to know your whereabouts. I find that although so far separated by time and distance we are still near together in some respects."[54]

There were additional interests. Berthoud participated actively in the founding and construction of Golden's Calvary Episcopal Church and became a charter, and semi-permanent, member of its vestry. One wonders if this were not really Helen's doing, for he still chose not to seek confirmation as an Episcopalian. He helped incorporate a paper mill. He drew up as a private exercise the first serious, large-scale map of Jefferson County. It was not a brilliant example of the graphic arts, for his penmanship was, as always, indelicate, but its accuracy was such that it could not possibly have been produced by an amateur.[55]

His diversions, of course, had by no means inhibited the usual pursuit of his profession. His remarkable personal energy contained unabated, and he remained unabashed by detail. The *Transcript* carried regular advertisements of his engineering offices on First Street. Nor were his professional activities confined to the environs of Golden. Most of the Rocky Mountain region was as yet unsurveyed in detail, and much of the remainder of his life would be spent in mapping it.

A considerable part of 1869 was devoted to projects for the General Land Office. The late spring saw him back in the Arkansas valley, recording the windings of the river between Pueblo and the future site downstream of Nepesta (his "meander lines" totaled 42 miles, 60 chains, and 48 links, and his stipend was $513). On July 12, he commenced, with two chainmen and an axeman, the subdivision of two foothills townships (Ranges 71 and 72 West of Number 5 South). It was strenuous work, yet intriguing; his field notes abounded with references to the high quality of the regional valley and park land — attractive sites for ranches and, in the next century, mountain suburbs. He commented in greater detail upon the local vegetation, and in particular upon the country rock, its intrusions and possible minerals. Perhaps his most startling observation was a flock of white-winged doves which he encountered in sub-Alpine surroundings on the upper reaches of Cub Creek. A "Lower Sonoran" variety typical of the warmer southwestern deserts, these birds were quite simply out of place. Berthoud "took" two of them, but failed to preserve their skins, which was unfortunate. Yet his reports passed muster with the authoritative Elliott Couse and later with the respected Colorado ornithologist Wells Woodbridge Cook; only a handful of latter-day pundits have raised serious eyebrows. It was, of course, another instance of Berthoud's penchant for rarities. On the other hand, as every experienced observer knows, many birds are capable of marvelous deviations from their normal habitats.[56]

The foothills survey was complete by July 28. It was Berthoud's final undertaking for the land office, and most of the long remainder of his career would be associated with the explosive private enterprise of his time and place. That much of it would have to do with the railroads was inevitable. And it was also a foregone conclusion that he would occasionally become involved in ventures as gossamer as the plumage of the Carolina parakeet.[57]

CHAPTER IV

The Colorado Central

"Broad is the way that leadeth to Golden, but
narrow is the gauge up Clear Creek canon."

Golden Globe, August 16, 1876

Golden continued infatuated with the iron horse. Although its
hopes for a transcontinental had been swept away amid the snows of
Rollins Pass, it still could seek a not-inconsiderable alternative, the
control, at Denver's expense, of the principal commerce of Colorado.

After passage of more than a century, this may sound absurd, but
in 1867, the notion seemed reasonable. The dominance of Denver
was by no means certain. Its seniority was slight; furthermore its location at the confluence of Cherry Creek and the South Platte River
gave no positive assurance of empire. Golden on the other hand lay
at the gateway to the most productive mining region in the southern
Rockies, precisely at the point where plains transit became mountain
transport. Furthermore, though the Union Pacific might shrink from
Colorado's great divide, it lusted after Colorado's ores. And the Union
Pacific was coming on fast; by November it would reach the recently
designated division point called Cheyenne. Why shouldn't Golden,
through which so many blessings already flowed, build a railroad direct
to a junction with the new transcontinental? The entombment of
Denver would then be complete.

This was the special dream of Bill Loveland, and all Golden proclaimed it valid. It already was legally certified by the charter of the Colorado Central; its financing might well be undertaken by the Union Pacific; and Captain Berthoud could trace it across the map. Enough said.

The Union Pacific, unfortunately, was only half-willing. It offered no money; it would, however, lay the track and provide the rolling stock, but the Colorado Central must survey the route, do the grading, and provide the Union Pacific with a first mortgage upon its *entire* property. It also was suggested, not quite so bluntly, that the Union Pacific influence on the Colorado Central board should be promoted into effective control.[1]

Berthoud was less hesitant. He shelved the insurance office, the territorial library and treasury, and the U.S. Department of State and began gathering men and equipment for a reconnaissance northward. His terms were minimal — a basic salary plus expenses.[2]

The year 1867 was one of Indian alarms, and the captain was issued six serviceable carbines from the nearest public stores. His initial problem was not Indians, however, but the early summer runoff from the adjacent mountains. St. Vrain Creek, he reported, had a "racehorse current," while the crossing of the Big Thompson required both swimming and boating. Nonetheless, trailside accounts of Indian depredations turned increasingly grave. Cheyennes and Arapahoes in unprecedented numbers were sweeping the plains to the east, butchering and burning. Six carbines seemed altogether inadequate, and at the Cache la Poudre River, Berthoud cut short his survey and turned abruptly homeward, following the conventional and heavily traveled route along the South Platte. He reappeared in Golden on the evening of July 19. Although somewhat disappointed, he remained hopeful; his alignment from Ralston Creek to the St. Vrain was technically flawless, while in the more difficult country beyond he had held his gradient to less than 1 percent. The total distance from Golden to the Poudre had come to fifty-eight miles.[3]

Golden too remained hopeful. Loveland was in the midst of brisk discussions with representatives of the Union Pacific, especially Colonel T. J. Carter, a Union Pacific director who already was spoken of as a suitable choice for the Colorado Central's presidency. Coached by Loveland, Carter took to the stump in behalf of a "mountain division" to the mines; Loveland urged financing by county bond issues, while Berthoud, greatly reinforced, resumed his northward reconnaissance.[4]

He departed again on August 6. This time he enjoyed the protection of ten veteran cavalrymen, suitably mounted and accoutered. As they jangled out of Golden, the *Transcript* predicted that such experienced borderers would have "little compunction of conscience so far as Indians were concerned." Once again, however, the tribesmen failed to appear, and Berthoud pushed his surveys routinely from the Poudre northeastward to Crow Creek, thence diagonally across the escarpment of the high plains to a junction with the freshly graded transcontinental line a short distance west of Cheyenne. On his return, he ran an alternative and rather more appropriate line by way of Box Elder Creek. Near the escarpment they came upon some distinctive fossil indications — shells and sharks' teeth from the Upper Cretaceous, the bones of "gigantic *carnivora* of the Tertiary," plus numerous aboriginal human remains. The little captain was predictably fascinated, and selected specimens, carefully labeled, went off to the Smithsonian.[5]

Berthoud, with his assistants and outriders, re-entered Golden on September 6. This time they were greeted without enthusiasm. The "Colorado Central" counties, Jefferson excepted, had refused to provide financial aid. The expenses of the survey had already totaled $50,000 and Berthoud certainly — and perhaps his staff as well — were compensated with promises of future payment. Bluntly stated, the Colorado Central lacked the means to establish its own alignment.[6]

Yet Golden could not simply wait for a more propitious season. Well-founded rumors hinted that Denver would very soon launch its own line to the north. On November 6, therefore, Loveland and Berthoud, bearing proposals, boarded a stage for Cheyenne, from which they continued by rail to the east. It was not a comfortable journey. The Union Pacific had as yet no regular passenger schedule, and indeed as late as 1870 the best published running time from Cheyenne to the Missouri River exceeded twenty-three hours. The dusty little coaches jostled atrociously over the unsettled track; there were lengthy delays beside the debris of recent construction; and an authentic Indian scare ran with them as far as Kearney, Nebraska. They did transact business in Omaha and probably in Chicago, and they may well have pushed farther to Boston, where a construction syndicate called the "Credit

A Colorado Central train steaming up Clear Creek Canyon. *Courtesy of the Colorado Historical Society.*

Mobilier" already presided over the destinies of the Union Pacific. In any case, Berthoud's surveys were approved and new ones authorized, and he even received cordial assurances as to the payment of his salary. He and Loveland were back in Golden well before the end of the month.[7]

One of the sanctioned routes penetrated the mountains by way of Clear Creek Canyon, and the captain had his surveyors at work on it as early as November 27. This time there was no thought of deluxe tunneling; the line would be of three-foot gauge and would follow the natural sinuosities of the defile. This would yield a manageable gradient, but only with curves quite unsuited to a standard-gauge railroad. It was the Festiniog idea, somewhat enlarged and applied to the Rockies, and Berthoud was presently commissioned to place 37,000 ties at various points in the canyon. There was as yet little publicity. "Bands of music, buncombe telegraphic dispatches and fancy envelopes never built a railroad," averred the *Golden Transcript*, "and never will." However, if buncombe was absent, so, still, was cash, and Berthoud received nineteen shares of company stock "worth" $400 in lieu of conventional pay.[8]

Even the buncombe appeared. The Kansas Pacific Railroad, whose corporate pedigree included Berthoud's old Leavenworth, Pawnee & Western, was building unsteadily westward; its goal was obviously Colorado, but for a number of intricate reasons it hesitated to establish a terminus in Denver. Bill Loveland was quick to perceive an opportunity. Why shouldn't the Colorado Central construct a short, standard-gauge spur direct from Golden to a meeting with the Kansas Pacific at a point *outside* of Denver? Why shouldn't *Golden* enjoy the advantages of gauge-to-gauge interchange on a completed route from the mines to the east? Why shouldn't Golden, where precious ores encountered coal, become the smelting center of America? All at the expense of Denver!

It would be easy — fifteen miles of standard gauge down lower Clear Creek and over the Platte to the Kansas Pacific. County securities would pay for it. Golden celebrated the New Year of 1868 with a premature ground-breaking, and "Cap" Berthoud, reportedly well-wined, joined in the exaggerations. His actual survey was of course more deliberate. But when the Denver press questioned the legality of a Jefferson County bond issue, he retorted sharply, and officially, as chairman of the Jefferson County Commissioners.

Golden, alas, was doomed to frustration. Already the territorial seat of government had been transferred — permanently — to Denver; moreover, Denver's own Denver Pacific Railroad was opened to Cheyenne on June 22, 1870, before the Colorado Central could so much as touch rails with the Kansas Pacific. The first Colorado Central train, on Saturday, September 24, 1870, told the story. It was a kind of interurban run, Denver to Golden, via the Denver Pacific to "Cut-Off Junction," then over the Colorado Central to its destination. Golden chose to overlook this, and another celebration was as lavish as specious expectations would make it. There were speeches. There were spikes of silver and gold. Toasts were offered to Gilpin County ("its undeveloped mineral wealth is sufficient to discharge the national debt"), to southern Colorado, to Omaha, to San Francisco, and, with a nod toward reality, to the Gas Works of Denver. Berthoud this time was not present; he was rumored to be examining the Ralston Creek coal measures with "two men and a boy."[9]

The hand of the Union Pacific, usually friendly, alway parental, and occasionally stern, seldom left the shoulder of the Colorado Central. The relations between the companies resembled a continually shuffled deck of cards, an interfacing of aspirations and personalities played out against such disparate backgrounds as Washington Street, Golden, and State Street, Boston. Boston officially dominated. The president of the Colorado Central was chosen in New England; a majority of its directors were New Englanders of Union Pacific affiliation; its secretary was E.H. Rollins, an energetic New Hampshireman turned Boston financier; and its chief engineer was for some years "General" T.C. Sickles, chief engineer of the Union Pacific.

Yet Boston's power was sometimes more formal than real. The New Englanders quickly discovered that a stable of Colorado surrogates was a convenience if not a necessity. The details — they were exceptionally complex — need not concern us. It is sufficient to observe that an early (post-Carter) Colorado Central president was the fast-rising Coloradoan, Henry M. Teller, that the executive vice-president was frequently Bill Loveland, and that Ed Berthoud sat occasionally on the board and repeatedly served as acting secretary and supervised nearly all of the civil engineering. The Bostonians went further. They placed on the Colorado Central board another well-known Goldenite named

Charles C. Welch. Welch was a man of adventurous background and entrepreneurial instincts. Like Berthoud he had been raised in upstate New York and was of nearly the same age. A series of youthful impulses had taken him to California, Australia, and twice around Cape Horn, and he had been a passenger in one of the tri-weekly stages that had rattled past the Berthouds westbound on the plains in the spring of 1860. Welch had inherited the black hair and ruddy complexion of a French-Canadian mother; his father's roots ran deep into seventeenth-century Massachusetts Bay. Through them both he had acquried the capabilities that go well with a developing country. [10]

By 1870, Berthoud had completed his canyon surveys, and early in 1871, a more hopeful outlook for the mining counties bade fair to assure the funds for actual construction. Further, a marked improvement in the national economy had resurrected Bill Loveland's Golden-to-Union Pacific dream, and the little captain shortly found himself involved with both undertakings. His personal energy continued undiminished, and his health remained superb. (He recently had survived and fully recovered from a twenty-foot plunge in an unanchored bucket down a coal mine shaft!) [11]

The canyon extension swiftly reconfirmed his narrow gauge thesis. Berthoud accurately estimated that construction costs would be less than one-half of those for a standard gauge line; the grading expenses actually came to no more than $20,000 per mile. The narrow gauge locomotives weighed at the most nine tons, which in turn permitted lighter rail — only twenty-five pounds to the yard. The width of embankments could be held to six feet. And the cost of a narrow gauge gondola car averaged no more than $307. Not only Gilpin, Jefferson, and Boulder counties, but also the New England tycoons, were greatly encouraged; all agreed to float loans. [12]

The work was "prosecuted vigorously." The first designated superintendent of the construction was T.C. Sickles of the Union Pacific, who quickly transferred his responsibilities to an eager volunteer, Second Lieutenant Frederick D. Grant, aged twenty-one, a recent graduate of the U.S. Military Academy. Grant had just been commissioned a cavalryman, and his engineering background was clearly limited, but he was an amiable young man and also a son of the President of the United States; he could not be shrugged aside. Berthoud naturally performed the actual supervising, and in Augsut 1871, he guided Sickles

A Colorado Central train at the forks of Clear Creek. *Courtesy of the Denver Public Library.*

and Grant over the whole canyon alignment. He had at his disposal a cadre of graders and track layers of the breed that built the West, and the work moved forward with a speed seldom matched in so awkward a terrain. Following eleven months of blasting and filling, the first rails went down at Golden on July 22, 1872. By August 31, they were at the "Big Hill," on September 15 at the "Forks," and just before Christmas reached a temporary terminus at Black Hawk. Already trains of ore and exursionists were filling the canyons with smoke.[13]

The happy picture had, to be sure, its flaws. Springtime floods washed out whole sections of roadbed. There were derailments with casualties. And though the upper mining towns had celebrated both Christmas and the railroad with gusto, they quickly learned to berate the railroad. Ore shippers desired a choice of destination, and they promptly demanded an inner third rail along the Colorado Central's standard gauge route to Denver, an arrangement that would permit unbroken narrow gauge operation from mine tipple to a variety of consignees. Golden naturally cherished its quasi-monopoly as a transfer point and fought stubbornly to prevent any change. Tempers grew short; the high country press turned sarcastic; Golden retorted in kind. The controversy continued for *seven years*. At last the Boston stockholders were driven to intervene. They opted for the uninterrupted haul, and the third rail was spiked down in December 1879. All Golden cried foul, but no one was more indignant than Berthoud. In a cooperative regional history, published the following year, he termed the New Englanders "dyspeptic," "bilious," and "flatulent" and denounced their action as "an exhibition of cheek and meddlesome importunity." It was rather unlike him.[14]

Nearly coincident with the canyon narrow gauge came the Golden-to-Union Pacific effort. It was given special encouragement by additional bond issues, and on August 24, 1871, a telegram from T.C. Sickles in Omaha instructed Berthoud to organize an immediate survey between Golden and Pine Bluffs, Wyoming, a station on the Union Pacific main line a few miles east of Cheyenne. Sickles furthermore specified a three-foot gauge, which may have been less a measure of Golden's influence than of Union Pacific parsimony. Berthoud as usual responded with vigor; he was in the field at the end of September, and his reconnaissance — which represented rather more than a modification of his original Crow Creek alignment — was completed in early November. At the start he shared formal responsibilities with Lieutenant Grant, but that pleasant young man soon departed on a six-month leave from which he never returned.[15]

In the course of 1872, the Pine Bluffs scheme was revised and enlarged into a *standard gauge* undertaking, Golden to Julesburg in the far northeast corner of Colorado, but likewise on the transcontinental line. Once again the captain handled the initial chores, commencing in May and concluding in September. He made use of his earlier surveys with moderate adjustments as far as Greeley, thence ran east and northeast down the South Platte, close to, but not always identical with, the later Union Pacific cutoff.[16]

The actual construction proceeded more slowly, and it was far from complete when the regional euphoria was brutally extinguished by the financial crash of September 1873. Yet it was, while it lasted, a major effort. The first earth was turned at "Golden Junction," two miles down the existing road toward Denver, on September 5, 1872, and by April 1873, a total of 250 teams and 400 men were at work at a variety of points. During the winter quantities of cross-ties were delivered along the road as far as Longmont, and the fifty-pound rails actually entered the town on April 16, just a day within the time-limit prescribed in the applicable Boulder County subsidy. On the 22nd, Colorado Central Locomotive Number 1 drew six coaches of invited guests, Berthoud included, over the first forty-one miles. It was a season of expectation. Already the line between Longmont and Greeley was ready for track, and grading parties were at work on the long tangents between Greeley and Julesburg. The work was pushed steadily all summer and imposed considerable responsibilities on Berthoud, for this phase involved more exacting procedures than the primary reconnaissance.[17]

Nor was this his only concern. Bill Loveland's fantasies had continued apace. If a Golden to Julesburg road would contribute to Denver's isolation, a modest narrow gauge extension from Golden southeasterly to the brand new (and narrow gauge) Denver & Rio Grande Railway would surely guarantee it. This brainstorm had recently been incorporated into a Golden & South Platte Railway and Telegraph Company, with Berthoud as its secretary and chief engineer. Its titular president was Charles C. Welch. Its relations with the Colorado Central were intimate.[18]

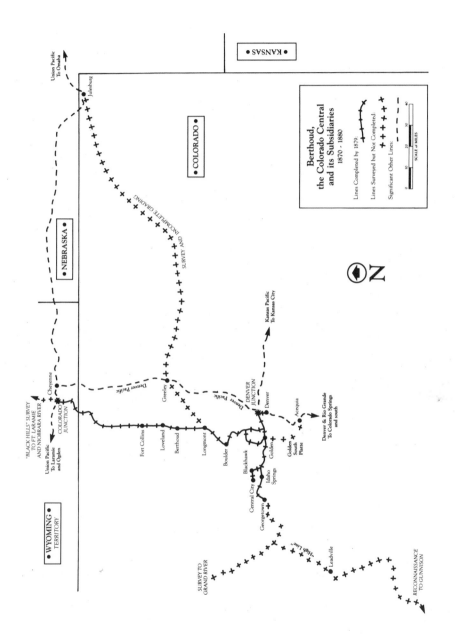

Berthoud,
the Colorado Central
and its Subsidiaries
1870 - 1880

Lines Completed by 1879:
Lines Surveyed but Not Completed:
Significant Other Lines:

SCALE of MILES
0   10   20   30   40

N

The career of the Golden & South Platte was to a large extent played out in a single year — 1873. This, plus the fact that Berthoud was its secretary, left many of its records among the captain's personal papers — records, it must be said, that were marred by a certain inelegance. Another bond election on January 17, 1873, in Jefferson County took care of the necessary subsidy, but the transactions were clearly manipulated and led to discourteous questions. Contractors and suppliers were paid with the bonds, which the primitive financial community promptly discounted at sixty to seventy-five cents on the dollar. But the county authorities remained friendly, the opposition disintegrated, and the road went forward. By mid-September the grading was finished, the bridges completed, and the cross-ties in place over the whole projected distance (to Acequia, near present Louviers). Rails and fastenings were accumulating at Golden, and the *Globe* was predicting that "the cars" would be running by October.[19]

Railroad building in the pioneer west was a risky business, and its promoters understood this perfectly well. In an effort to hold themselves personally harmless they resorted to a variety of tactics, of which a favorite was the "in house" construction company, a device by which they could contract — often very profitably — to build their own railroads. The management of the Union Pacific had such a company, the famous (or infamous) Credit Mobilier. But the entrepreneurs of Golden had two: the Colorado Improvement Company and the Jefferson Construction Company. The former had responsibility for the line from Longmont to Julesburg and was administered by Welch; the latter embraced the Longmont to Golden to Acequia segments and was managed by Berthoud.[20]

The Jefferson Construction Company was legally organized on April 5, 1873; its stated purposes were railroad, wagon road, and telegraph development, plus real estate acquisitions and sales. Officially, Berthoud was an incorporator and trustee, but essentially he ran the enterprise, negotiating the subcontracts, ordering materials, and conducting surveys. The relations between the several companies, both railroad and construction, were everywhere imprecise, and funds flowed between them without the slightest impediment. The county bonds served practically as currency, and as they passed by stages to the final subcontractors they incurred, as noted, substantial discounts. A preferred indebtedness was, however, met with cash — things like office

A Colorado Central train on the Mountain City bridge near Central City.
Courtesy of the Denver Public Library.

rent in Loveland's business block and the expense of the January bond referendum. The latter was technically the business of the Golden & South Platte, yet the receipts for payment were filed away, presumably by Berthoud, among the records of the construction company. They reveal certain peccadillos: the moneys expended by individual stockholders, including Berthoud; the charges for "cigars and refreshments;" a saloon bill "for Judges and Others;" a livery invoice for "horses and care of horses, election;" and a sum of $100 paid to a public official (Patrick Desmond) "for services rendered during Bond Election." Together they provide an insightful statement in microcosm of contemporary political mores. Berthoud as secretary-treasurer made no effort to disguise them.[21]

He ran, quite simply, with the approved enthusiasms. He even found time to prepare a brochure on the Colorado Central; though entitled an "Itinerary," it was in fact a gazetteer of towns, villages, and resources, laced with statistics, legends, and wildlife. He echoed all the regional bombast; everywhere (except for Denver!) he stressed the local beauty, salubrity, and prosperity. He presented oddities: an Indian skull from Clear Creek Canyon that was reputed to be of Aztec origin; the "Siberian Squirrel, tail-less and earless" that dwelt at lofty elevations (this was of course the pika or coney); and an Indian legend of a "manhorse" that inhabited a lake close to Longs Peak. "Is this," he asked, "evidence of Indo-Greek tradition revived by a lousy [sic] Arapahoe . . . ?" His quoted altitudes above sea-level deserve notice. He cited 13,767 feet for Longs Peak and 10,914 for his pass, "as ascertained by the spirit level . . . by the Omaha datum line." Both were about 400 feet too low, and one may suspect a kind of spiritual lapse somewhere between Omaha and the mountains.[22]

Golden's extravaganza was part of a nationwide overindulgence, but it was more than usually unsound. It already has been noted that Berthoud's salary with the Colorado Central was not always paid in cash. The personal visit and patronage of President U.S. Grant on April 30, 1873, yielded widespread publicity, but minimal revenues. The thousand-and-one expenses of the Black Hawk extension became increasingly unmanageable, and late in August the treasurer of Jefferson County ordered the seizure of Colorado Central narrow gauge locomotive Number 5 for nonpayment of taxes. Far worse was the case of the Golden & South Platte. Its authorized capital was $400,000, but only

A Colorado Central train on switchback between Black Hawk and Central City. *Courtesy of the Colorado Historical Society.*

$126,000 had actually been subscribed. By September the company was unable to meet the wagon rental of Berthoud's surveyors, and its banker, F.E. Everett of Golden, was warning of overdrafts.[23]

The great eastern financial panic of September 17, 1873, revealed the truth, and the truth made Golden bankrupt. Within a week construction everywhere was suspended. Between Longmont and Julesburg more than a hundred miles of freshly graded roadbed were abandoned, trackless, to the plains. Timbers for a score of bridges were left on site to bleach; few were ever reclaimed. At Golden Berthoud was left with a small moraine of Golden & South Platte track fastenings — all debited to his personal account — and he considered himself fortunate to place them with the Colorado Central in return for depreciated county bonds. It was an irony that this transaction made possible the supreme indignity — the extension, in the fall of 1874, of the Colorado Central's own rails into *Denver*. It was a humiliating genuflexion, but it saved the desperate little carrier $500 per month in trackage fees.[24]

The effects of the crash lingered for months — and then for years. The Golden & South Platte confined itself to legal notices. To the northeast, the Colorado Central shrank back into Longmont; in the canyons it marked time.[25]

But the most alarming developments involved ownership and management. Although much of the Colorado Central's day-by-day administration had been conducted in Golden, a majority of its shares still were held in and about Boston. Moreover, the "principal" offices of the company were identical with those of the Union Pacific — also in Boston. The interests of Golden were clearly subject to change without notice. In addition, during the 1870s the name "Union Pacific" smacked of chicanery. The enormity of the Credit Mobilier scandal had by now come fully to the attention of the public; furthermore, any hope of early financial stability was ended by the election to the Union Pacific board in 1874 of the controversial financier, Mr. Jay Gould.[26]

Gould was a complicated person. To simply state that he was "bad" is to oversimplify. An impeccable family man, he seems also to have been a considerate private employer, and for this we have the testimony of both Grenville Dodge and Edward Berthoud. But his marketplace procedures were another matter, and he applied them without mercy and very profitably to the manipulation of railroads. "His brain was a network of them," remarked one of Berthoud's collegues, and among railroads he speculated, proxy and share, in the promotion of empire.[27]

Mr. Gould's manipulations had recently been focused upon the Kansas Pacific and Union Pacific. The details are of Byzantine complexity, but it may be said that he first arranged a pitiless competition between them and then an association. Each phase rewarded him hugely, but the profits of association were greater. Combination was already a favorite Gould technique, and it was inevitable that he should perceive the Colorado Central as a promising target for merger. The union was duly solemnized, as of December 8, 1875, by resolution of the Colorado Central's own directors, gathered in Golden; any local loyalties were quite overwhelmed by a barrage of eastern proxies. It was voted that the Colorado Central should be leased permanently to the Kansas Pacific, which now meant the Union Pacific, which meant Jay Gould. In addition, any Colorado residents holding Colorado Central stock were "invited" to tender their shares at 20 percent of par in return for the bonds of the original sponsoring counties at par.[28]

The intensity of the revolution was felt in other ways. Henry M. Teller was retained as president, but only, as before, as a figurehead. The Kansas Pacific sent out its own superintendent, Cyrus W. Fisher, who brought with him a bevy of replacements, train crews included, and it soon became evident that the interests of Golden and its neighboring counties were no longer of serious concern. Golden was indignant, and so were the counties. Inevitably, the scene was confused by local politicians; Colorado Democrats pointed to Teller, a Republican, and suggested a plot; Colorado Republicans hinted (on the whole incorrectly) that Jay Gould habitually hob-nobbed with Democrats. All parties agreed, however, that something must be done.[29]

Action was not long in coming. Late in April 1876, President Teller called a general meeting of the Colorado Central stockholders for May 18 in Golden, which was still by no means unusual, and it also was announced that Captain E.L. Berthoud would act as secretary in the absence, in Boston, of Edward H. Rollins; this too, had ample precedent. Nor was anything out of the ordinary expected. The Union Pacific alone controlled 7,200 of the 13,300 Colorado Central shares, and these were to be voted in person by Edward W. Rollins, the likeable young son of Edward H. In accordance with corporate bylaws, the Union Pacific proxies were delivered directly to Berthoud several days in advance of the meeting.[30].

As Berthoud routinely examined the certificates, the little captain perceived an electrifying opportunity. The elder Rollins had committed a monumental error; he had failed to provide his son with any formal authority to vote the Union Pacific's shares. Berthoud conveyed this crucial information, not to young Rollins, but to W.A.H. Loveland, and when the stockholders assembled on the morning of May 18, the Colorado partisans were prepared for a minor revolution. In the absence of Teller (another frequent situation), Loveland himself took the chair; the Boston proxies were instantly challenged and, with technical propriety, declared null and void. A completely new slate of directors was installed, heavily weighted with Coloradoans and with Loveland, Welch, and Berthoud atop the list. At an afternoon session the gleeful westerners adopted resolution upon resolution, ending the union with the Kansas Pacific, re-establishing their "principal" office in Golden, directing the transfer of the company seal and archives from Boston to Colorado, and striking down every expostulation that the unfortunate young Edward Rollins could make.[31]

The new directors went further. At the conclusion of the regular sessions, they moved across Clear Creek to hold a secluded conclave in Loveland's private office. Their decisions were crisp. They replaced the entire Colorado Central executive department. Loveland became president and Berthoud secretary, and Kansas Pacific heads rolled en masse down to the level of master mechanic. From the ousted and the outvoted they demanded records and papers, and to the surviving rank and file they prescribed obedience. No resistance, they warned, would be tolerated.[32]

The Kansas Pacific officials refused to budge. Superintendent Fisher at once instructed his employees not to obey the new regime, and he was supported, by telegraph, by President Teller. The Kansas Pacific treasurer, a rising Denverite named David H. Moffat, declined to turn over the company funds, and a formal demand upon Fisher to vacate the premises was met with a curt rejection.[33]

Again the Loveland group wasted no time. They held another secret conference and on the afternoon of Sunday, May 21, took physical action. At about 4:00 p.m., a half-hour before the arrival and departure of the evening passenger trains, a casual array of individuals crossed the bridge toward the Golden passenger station; among them were

GOLDEN

A woodcut of a Colorado Central train steaming out of Golden. *Courtesy of the Denver Public Library.*

Loveland, Berthoud, and their own carefully selected superintendent, Oren H. Henry. From the bridge they deployed to occupy the executive offices, roundhouse, and car shops. There was almost no violence. The onlookers were heavily of the local persuasion, and most of the incoming crewmen, conductors, and enginemen, pledged allegiance on the spot. A few were discharged summarily; one hopeless intractable had to be "helped" from his cab. The whole operation required less than thirty minutes. All company papers were secured intact. "Berthoud," reported Loveland, "executed his instructions to the letter." Golden was delirious. "New Broom Sweeps Clean," chortled the *Transcript*, "Loveland's Way Station again the Headquarters and Center of Attraction."[34]

For the moment Boston was helpless, and the younger Rollins, following a public outburst, accepted the situation and even agreed to serve the new management as temporary cashier. But the event could not be shrugged off, and lawsuits came quickly from Oakes and Oliver Ames, manipulators extraordinary, in Boston and from Gould in New York. The proceedings were conducted with an impressive complexity, but at last, on August 12, they produced the appointment of David Moffat as receiver in bankruptcy for the Colorado Central. Moffat's formal commissioning was set for August 15 at an appearance before Judge Amherst W. Stone of the Colorado Second Judicial District, sitting at the county courthouse in Boulder. Certain interested parties noted immediately that August 15 was the final day of the current judicial term.[35]

The response of the Golden group was once again swift. Early on the 14th, an emergency meeting of Loveland's board ordered a legal counter-attack, charging fraud and seeking the recovery of all Colorado Central bonds and shares still in the hands of the Union Pacific. But Golden — very quietly and to this day without absolute proof — prepared to go much farther. On the following morning, which was August 15, the regular Colorado Central passenger train from Denver to Boulder was brought to an unexpected halt before a barrier of cross-ties, and one of its passengers, who was none other than Judge Stone, was briskly removed from the cars at gun point and driven off toward the foothills in a light, fast carriage. There, behind a curtain wall of Dakota Sandstone, he was regaled for hours with milk, raspberries, and old Bourbon. Not until midnight had extinguished his authority was he conducted by masked outriders to Golden, where he was handed into a comfortable private conveyance and driven to his home in Denver.[36]

It was the first serious affront to the dignity of the new (August 1, 1876) State of Colorado, and the reaction of the authorities was as massive as it was fruitless. We read of a special troop train, trailing a field gun upon a flat car, and of swarms of Denver deputies. These the local officials, county and railroad, effectively neutralized by asking questions. The sheriff of Jefferson County was discovered, fly rod in hand, in the depths of Bear Creek Canyon, while Loveland, Welch, and Berthoud countered the uproar with carefully perfected bewilderment. At Boulder, a questionable hearing before a substitute judge produced, according to the *Transcript*, no more than "judicial expectoration." A fresh array of lawsuits befogged the issue, and Loveland's group, Berthoud included, remained in control for months, happily managing their little railroad and in fact substantially improving its operating results. (During the autumn they initiated inquiries into the new Westinghouse air brake.)[37]

No effective punishment was ever imposed; no one seemed able to identify the culprits. Judge Stone himself assumed a realistic attitude: "These boys," he announced, "treated me very nice; I am afraid if they get into trouble they will take me on another ride, and it won't be as pleasant as the first one." Berthoud's secretarial records were models of imprecision, and for the vital director's meeting of August 14 he simply indicated a "quorum." He did conduct a tedious correspondence with the United States Post Office Department, seeking a diversion, direct to Golden, of moneys due upon mail contracts, and at one point he charged his Union Pacific equivalent, E.H. Rollins, with "false pretenses." He later offered to apologize, but only if Rollins would cease his "meddling." His concurrent personal correspondence, such as it was, dealt with a technical monograph upon the St. Gotthard Tunnel, 5,000 miles away in the high Alps.[38]

It is likely that Berthoud's role in this extraordinary affair did not perfectly fulfill accepted standards of business conduct — even those in the 1870s. The Golden press justified him by abusing the Union Pacific; he himself said nothing. It may, of course, be suggested that his behavior was not inconsistent with that of his associates and that he played, as usual, a subordinate part. Nevertheless, his apparent transgressions were not widely admired — even at that high noon of American laissez-faire. About four years later, a respected regional commentator declared that the transactions of 1876 "did not redound greatly to the credit of Colorado railway management, and perhaps the less said about them the better." And indeed they seem never to have been mentioned again.[39]

*   *   *

Acts of piracy seldom lend themselves to viable conclusions; yet, the malfeasances of Loveland, Welch, and Berthoud ultimately did so, melding into a special set of circumstances to produce a surprisingly workable result. The year 1876 was a transitional one — nationally toward financial recovery, in Colorado toward profitable mining. Almost simultaneously, however, the comfortable marriage of the Denver, Union, and Kansas Pacific lines fell into unexpected disarray, a development that threatened to deprive the Union Pacific of much of its Colorado traffic. On the other hand, Loveland and his Colorado Central remained dangerously exposed to legal retribution. The sum of all the factors suggested an accommodation between the interests.[40]

It came rather suddenly. In February 1877, the Union Pacific lawsuits reached the United States Supreme Court, and Loveland was forced to give bond for $500,000. At the same time, the steadily improving mining economy again suggested a major expansion of the Colorado Central — west to Georgetown and Central City and, for a third time, north to the Union Pacific transcontinental. Meanwhile, the Kansas Pacific, like a cast-off spouse, was bruising the Union Pacific with a rate war. Amid these varied pressures Bill Loveland left for the east, bearing Berthoud's latest engineering data. The negotiations, conducted in Boston and New York, were brief, realistic, and without recrimination, and by March 10, an agreement, provisional but fundamental, had been reached. All pending lawsuits were dropped, the claims of Mr. Moffat annulled, and the de facto Golden directors for the time being retained. In addition, the Union Pacific would help with any reasonable Colorado Central expansion, the northerly line in particular. It was understood, however, that the Colorado Central would be operated in the Union Pacific interest, *pending further reorganization.*[41]

So prompt a conclusion had not been foreseen. On the night of March 9, "Prof. and Mrs." Berthoud had joined with the Golden directors to give an elaborate ball in honor of their chosen superintendent, Oren H. Henry; it was attended by representative citizens from Golden, Boulder, and the mountain towns, and they waltzed the hours away beneath a large banner: "The People of the Counties will stand by the C.C.R.R. as it is." But on the following evening Berthoud was handed a terse telegram from Loveland in New York: "Commence survey at once from Longmont to Cheyenne indirect by way of Fort

Collins." The particulars of the agreement became available on March 13. That they might be damaging to the Golden interests was not at first understood.[42]

Berthoud was back in the field within five days. His reconnaissance deviated little from his Box Elder route of 1867 and despite a late spring was carried rather quickly to completion. The "location" work, with its detailed stakings, was of course more time-consuming, and at Ryan's Crossing of the Big Thompson River there was another encounter with the seasonal runoff. It was, in truth, a near-disaster. A frigid flush of unexpected power overturned Berthoud's principal wagon, spilling personnel and equipment into the torrent; two of the party nearly lost their lives, while their surveying equipment — transits, levels, rods, and stakes — was swept completely away. Two of the younger men, carefully pre-heated with "Old Crow," endeavored to retrieve it, but in vain. Following a seven-day campout to await replacements, the party proceeded more comfortably, though there were skunks at the Cache la Poudre and rattlesnakes near the Box Elder. The former were discouraged with unlaundered human clothing, the latter with hatchets. At the high plains escarpment, close to Wyoming and the Union Pacific, Pikes Peak became visible with exceptional clarity, 140 miles away. And from a wheatfield near Longmont came Berthoud's *final* report of the Carolina parakeet![43]

The stakings hardly finished the business. Space for stations, sidings, and water tanks had to be provided; these for obvious reasons were commonly adjacent to streams. The facilities beside the Big Thompson were given Loveland's name, those by the Little Thompson Berthoud's; both would grow into attractive towns. Berthoud, Colorado, did experience a slight relocation, and the captain himself never developed a conspicuous interest in its affairs. His portrait, however, still hangs (1983) on the walls of its municipal library.[44]

There was a good deal more that season; indeed, 1877 was one of Berthoud's busiest. The grading and bridging, from Wyoming to Longmont, required constant supervision, and it also was pressured. The work got underway on July 20, and the entire line, seventy-seven miles in length, was opened to traffic on November 7. Westward in the mountains the narrow gauge went forward up the broadening valley to Georgetown; it closely followed Berthoud's earlier surveys, but likewise required oversight. Finally, at year's end, an awkward switch-

Berthoud, Colorado, in the 1980s showing the line originally surveyed by Berthoud a century earlier for the Colorado Central Railroad. *Courtesy of Robert C. Black, III.*

back reached toward Central City — a curiosity much cited as an engineering feat, but actually a compromise between a relentless terrain and a limited budget. [45]

The Colorado Central acted in 1877 as its own contractor, but its costs were underwritten, thanks to the "accommodation," by the Union Pacific, and the Union Pacific's own resources were far from limitless; in fact, a large portion of them consisted of watered securities. It was a precarious, possibly unethical, situation, yet Jay Gould was not a manipulator solely, and his transactions were by no means confined to his mansion at 578 Fifth Avenue, New York. He followed the progress of the Wyoming extension in person, and it soon became clear that his interest in the Colorado Central ran considerably deeper than that of a traditional absentee speculator. But if his presence assured the extensions, it also side-tracked Golden. Early in the spring of 1878, the Colorado Central's construction debts were funded by an additional issue of its own bonds, endorsed to the Union Pacific, and in March its entire physical property was leased outright to the Union Pacific for fifty years. The Colorado Central directors, Goldenites or no, could do little else.[46]

This meant, of course, an end to Loveland's personal dream. The triumph of the "east," if not of Denver, was complete. Nevertheless the displacement of the Coloradoans was carried out in a gentlemanly manner. Berthoud continued as the Colorado Central's secretary into June and as principal engineer into August, and he remained on the board of the company's Wyoming subsidiary to the end of 1880. Neither he nor Loveland wrung his hands in public; if they had lost their offices, they had acquired their trackage. As for Golden, the little city ignored defeat and pretended victory, and Loveland and Berthoud were publicly congratulated for arranging the transfer of so vital an enterprise to the capable hands of Mr. Gould![47]

CHAPTER V

Colorado Central's Children —
and Other Pursuits

The year 1878 was Berthoud's busiest year.

On the Colorado Central the influence of Jay Gould continued paramount. Nevertheless, Mr. Gould's financial appetites had suddenly been diverted toward an array of mining bonanzas that did not lie in Colorado at all, but in the Black Hills of Dakota Territory and among the complicated Rockies of southwestern Montana. Under the circumstances the wishes of Gould were the interests of Berthoud, and the captain quickly found himself involved with two extensive out-of-state projects, one of which was essentially unrelated to the Colorado Central.

His initial assignment established the pattern. He was to run a preliminary Colorado Central extension from Cheyenne, Wyoming, toward the Black Hills — to Fort Laramie certainly and as far beyond as time and circumstances permitted. Berthoud departed as quickly as he dared. By April 6, he had assembled a "full outfit" and two days later started north from a pre-established datum on the outskirts of Cheyenne. His party was unusually well-qualified. He had the assistance of Edward L. Jones, a youthful veteran of 1877, and we find for the first time the name of T.J. (Thomas Jefferson) Milner, a young graduate engineer with a long future in the Rocky Mountain West.[1]

The terrain was of the Great Plains variety, but the moderate surface was interrupted in many places by gullies, and the final descent to the Laramie River involved some undeniably difficult country. The weather was of the Wyoming springtime sort, and the men endured a steady succession of fronts. But the expedition, with data in five field books, rattled onto the parade ground at Fort Laramie as early as May 5.

Berthoud continued onward, possibly alone. Although he had recently turned fifty, he still thought nothing of *tours de force* on horseback, and he pressed a rapid personal reconnaissance to the valley of the "Eau qui Court" (Niobrara), many miles to the northeast and close to Dakota itself. It was clearly a feat of speed and endurance, for he subsequently got his notes, equipment, and personnel back to Golden on the night of May 12. "The Captain and his party," observed a local reporter, "are looking pretty rough for men who claim to have any pretensions to civilization."[2]

His results were promising. His suggested line from Cheyenne to Fort Laramie was ninety-one miles in length with a maximum gradient of eighty feet to the mile (1.52 percent). Assuming thirty-ton locomotives on fifty-pound rails he estimated a total cost of $915,497.80 for permanent way and buildings. But the Colorado Central, and Jay Gould, had expected to pay for the road with the bonds of the City of Cheyenne, and when the municipal fathers there demurred, the project ground to a halt. It would never be put through as intended.

Jay Gould was a born speculator, but the Cheyenne incident suggested that in a special way he was also a prudent man, and he typically was eager that his risks should be assumed by others. It was partly for this reason that Montana continued to attract his attention. Its mining booms at Butte Hill and Helena had substance, and its territorial legislature was abuzz with talk of railroad subsidies. Furthermore, an actual railhead, convenient of access and suitable for extension, already existed. It was called the Utah Northern. It was of the less expensive three-foot gauge, and it ran from Ogden, the western terminus of Gould's own Union Pacific, to Franklin, astride the boundary of Idaho Territory. (As an *insolvent* Morman cooperative it may have been unique.) It was natural prey for Mr. Gould, and he secured possession of the property, by way of the sheriff's hammer, in April 1878. Thereafter he wasted no time. He modified its name to Utah & Northern, and construction gangs, primed with Union Pacific promises, thrust the spindly trackage northward for more than forty miles. By early June, they were at a company encampment called Oneida. There they paused; beyond was essential wilderness, devoid of dependable data.[4]

Gould traveled west, examined the situation, and called for Berthoud. Again the captain responded. He sent Helen off on a two-month junket with eastern relatives, supplemented his field force with Colorado Central office personnel, and re-staffed the Colorado Central with faculty members from the fledgling Colorado School of Mines (To the faculty members he lent a theodolite and a telescope with which to observe a total eclipse of the sun, predicted for the afternoon of July 29.) His surveyors soon were steaming across Wyoming, and all hands assembled at Oneida before the end of June.[5]

Oneida (it no longer specifically exists) was an array of tents and shacks, sited among willows. It bustled sturdily, but amid its chuffings and bumpings it was profoundly worried. All Idaho as well as adjacent Montana lay that summer in the grip of a serious Indian scare. The incredible fighting retreat of Chief Joseph and his Nez Percé was a recent and vivid memory, and now there were encounters with Bannocks, frequently on a combat basis. Berthoud in fact requested a military escort, but the army held back, citing priorities, and the best he could do was equip himself with rifles of an advanced pattern and to remind his men that they were of course good shots. Golden, too, was aware of the danger. "It looks like a pretty scaly trip," the *Transcript* remarked. "Good-bye, boys. Take care of yourselves."[6]

The expedition could at least take comfort in numbers. The survey team totaled seventeen; nearly all were veterans. Thanks to surviving vouchers, we can list their specialties: resident engineer (T.J. Milner), levelers (including the bright young Jones), chainmen, flagmen, axemen, laborers, and a cook. Their pay was by no means handsome. Berthoud's monthly salary was $350, Milner's, $140; the others received between $40 and $45. Camp-shelter and board were of course also provided. There was furthermore a contract freighter, James Packer, who brought six pair of draft horses, four wagons, three drivers, and three saddle horses, all for $18 per day. Together they made an impression. The Indians at Fort Hall Agency watched them sullenly, but they passed through unmolested and presently were encamped beside the Ross fork of the Snake River. Here the map became an essential void and their serious work began. It was the Fourth of July, and they embellished their notebooks with penciled United States flags.[7]

Berthoud knew that the country ahead was arid and that the passes were moderate, but he did not yet appreciate how arid — or how moderate. The Idaho plains were a succession of sand and lava fields, sometimes stubbled with sage, but often nearly devoid of vegetation. In the distant east were hints of Tetons, but the sun blazed relentlessly down, and the only shade was cast by the poles of a recently erected telegraph line. Berthoud considered the region "Phlegiaean" [Phlegettontic] and "doomed to eternal sterility." But his surveyors measured nearly ten miles of it each day, and the continental divide beyond seemed, by Colorado standards, an engineer's dream. Pleasant Valley (Monida) Pass was a "mere wrinkle;" there was some 2 ½ percent grade in a respectable canyon, but on July 22 they established their bench mark upon the summit — 6855.98 feet above the sea. The opposite slope carried them without incident into comparative verdure, and on the evening of the 23rd they camped beside the clear and copious waters of Red Rock Creek.[8]

They were in high spirits. Young Jones closed out his number-two level book with a private flourish: "Thus endeth the First Lesson of the Second Book," to which the captain appended, in classic Greek, "End of the Second Book of Berthoud for Leveling." Their route continued straightforward. The Red Rock became the Beaverhead and the Beaverhead the Jefferson, all of them upon an evenly descending water grade. But Berthoud was a thorough man, and on the Red Rock he divided his company, dispatching flankers eastward to investigate the Stinking Water.[9]

The main body did encounter some narrows, but these were in no way comparable to Colorado's Clear Creek Canyon, and on the morning of July 29 the party found itself at Ryan's, a kind of stage station plus hay ranch, nestled close to the Beaverhead beneath jumbled crags. Here they paused for the predicted eclipse of the sun.[10]

The solar eclipse of July 29, 1878, was very widely observed, for the moon's shadow raced down the whole axis of the Rockies, from northwest to southeast, through a nearly faultless summer afternoon. Berthoud, as might have been expected, approached it in the fashion of an engineer. He established an observation point (it was probably across the river from the present "Pipe Organ Rock") and determined the altitude and latitude by spirit level and solar observation. Under wilderness circumstances he could make only an estimate of his longitude. But his data for the eclipse, expressed in apparent local solar time, are probably highly accurate; included are the four "contacts" and the duration of totality, two minutes, fifty-six seconds.[11]

Figures provided the substance of Berthoud's comments. He did record the wind direction, the temperature of the air, and condition of the sky. He noted also that swarms of grasshoppers — a summertime specialty in this region — dropped to the ground at the beginning of totality. But of the majesty of this finest of natural spectacles he contributed not a word.[12]

The eclipse was unrecorded in his official survey books, and his men resumed their leveling at once. They now maintained a special alert, for the Indian scare had emptied the local ranches, and near the mouth of the Beaverhead one of Berthoud's marksmen knocked over a skulking Bannock — who turned out to be a tree stump. But their nervousness did have justification, and at Salisbury Post Office the entire party, flankers included, joined a cluster of settlers to improvise defenses. It was here on the late evening of August 5 that the captain climbed aboard a southbound stage, enroute for Oneida and Golden.[13]

He took a calculated risk; the first 150 miles or so were by now dangerously exposed to Indian attack, but he deemed it vital to get his existing data to a place of safety. Futhermore, it was time for his engineer-professors at Golden to start converting them to profiles. His gamble paid off. His coach was unmolested, and seven nights and ten meals later he was in Golden. Nor did his field party tarry long in Salisbury; by his specific orders, and under Milner's supervision, they continued eastward and northward across the intricate, but on the whole adaptable, terrain, and on the evening of August 17 they established their final bench mark beside the principal school house in Helena.[14]

Berthoud remained in Golden until August 24. He became entangled in administrative matters; moreover Jay Gould suddenly saw fit to groom him, by telegraph, as a confidential political agent. Gould's Montana manipulations were already well advanced. At Helena, he was in intimate touch with Samuel T. Hauser, an engineer by training, a banker in fact, and, by avocation, a public lobbyist. Through Hauser and the regional press, Gould rang the changes for subsidies; he promised action, threatened delays, and hinted that his railroad could easily be diverted elsewhere. To Berthoud he first proposed an appraisal of mining properties, but the crux of his strategy was contained in a message on August 17: "While you are in Montana I would like to have you lay the foundation for an Act of the legislature exempting us from taxation and one million to twelve hundred thousand dollars of County Bonds . . ." Additional wires reached Berthoud in the course of his return; the last, received at Oneida, raised the specter of a revised terminus in Washington Territory.[15]

From Oneida the Montana stage carried him northward through continuing rumors. Yet again, there were no Bannocks; his coach was either a rolling arsenal or else very lucky, for the journey was accomplished without incident, and Berthoud was in Helena by the evening of the 30th. He found his men scattered over several river valleys, but he at least could telegraph their friends that their scalps were intact. There is no evidence that he sought out the formidable Hauser or laid any "foundation" for public assistance; in any case, the territorial legislature was not in session. He was, to be sure, taken in hand by a certain Martin Maginnis, a balding worthy who could fairly be called Mr. Montana Democrat. The captain, however, appears to have confined himself entirely to civil, rather than political, engineering.[16]

He did engage in a number of related activities: mineralogic, topographic, and even social. He investigated at least eight mining camps, setting off in the process a flurry of hopeful editorials. He was specially impressed by Helena; he proclaimed it (in tune with the gospel of Golden) superior to Denver, and in truth the little city fairly overwhelmed him with hospitality. But much of this was arranged by the regional U.S. Army paymaster, Major John E. Blaine, whom Berthoud had known in Leavenworth; the political nuances, if any, were unclear.[17]

It was late in September when Berthoud finally reassembled his surveyors at the mouth of the Madison River and set out southward, by curves and tangents, toward Raynald's Pass. They moved with some urgency as reports of Indians still drifted in over the ranges, and at the top of the continental divide they were spattered by the season's first snowfall. But the pass proved another engineer's delight, and just beyond, at Henry's Lake, a sequence of meadows beckoned them eastward into Yellowstone National Park. The park jaunt had in fact been prescribed. Jay Gould, whose appreciation of tourist dollars surpassed his respect for conservation, was openly toying with the idea of a direct inter-geyser railroad service.[18]

Berthoud's party remained in Yellowstone for nearly a week, and everyone enjoyed it immensely. They were much amused when a government expedition-in-residence mistook them for hostile Bannocks and took to the timber, and they were greatly pleased when the fugitives turned out to be a division of the Hayden Survey under the highly-regarded A.C. Peale; it guaranteed elegant campfire discourse. The weather continued raw, but they slept comfortably in their buffalo robes, and the thermal vapors were luxuriant. The regional birdlife was deficient in species (only fifteen by Berthoud's count), but the geysers behaved most handsomely. There were full-dress displays, not only of the Castle and Old Faithful, but also of Giant and Giantess. Moreover, unhindered by public authority, they thrust a selected lodgepole pine into the mouth of Old Faithful and sat back to watch. The result surpassed all expectations — the tree soared heavenward, amid steam and turmoil, for more than sixty feet.[19]

The rest of their survey was, by contrast, denouement. From Henry's Lake the north fork of the Snake gave them some technical trouble, and they continued to worry over Indians, but within a few days, at Beaverhead Canyon, they triumphantly intersected their original alignment and packed away their instruments. The desert beyond was less forbidding in October than in July, and on the 20th they met the advancing Utah & Northern railhead. Thereafter they rode the cars, devouring freshly harvested fruit. Most of them, including Berthoud, reached Golden on the evening of September 22.[20]

They were greeted warmly; among the welcomers was Helen, recently returned from the east. But the survey was not over; the final conversion of field data to maps, profiles, and estimates kept Berthoud and six assistants busy, chiefly at Golden, until the end of November, and Berthoud himself traveled to New York for personal discussions with Gould. His final report was elaborate (and encouraging), and he was able to deliver it complete for a total cost to Gould of $10,195.02. In addition, the 1878 dollar, a comparatively reasonable terrain, and a certain tendency to optimism on Berthoud's part produced an estimate for grading, Ross Fork to Helena, 323 miles, of $435,000, or just $1,346 per mile.[21]

Gould was jubilant, and when the Department of the Interior presumed to delay his passage across the Fort Hall Reservation, he merely shrugged it aside. Yet he continued to expect his Montana tax exemption, and this he did not get; the territorial governor, B.F. Potts, though Republican and sympathetic, was efficiently frustrated by a newly elected Democratic legislature. Gould soon abandoned his active interest in the Utah & Northern and turned his talents elsewhere; though a stubborn man, he rarely clung to what he felt was a lost cause. On the other hand the Utah & Northern did continue forward; an alternate group on the Union Pacific board could not bear to abandon so intriguing an effort. The rails reached Butte and Helena, generally upon Berthoud's alignments, in 1881, and were extended to Garrison, Montana, well to the north, in 1884. With a line mileage of nearly 500, it was for a time one of the longest narrow gauge railroads in the world. It was converted to standard gauge during 1890-91 and was eventually absorbed into the Union Pacific System. It would even reach Yellowstone Park, though never the cone of Old Faithful. [22]

*   *   *

The Utah & Northern was never, even through the person of Mr. Gould, a close relative of the Colorado Central, but another and nearly simultaneous undertaking was. It carried a succession of corporate names, but was invariably known in Golden as the "High Line." It was to run directly across the topographic grain of the Colorado Rockies from Georgetown (via a pass that carried Bill Loveland's name) to Leadville and beyond. Save for a famous initial stretch, it was never to be built at all. As an embryo, however, it developed — at least on paper — some elaborate arms and legs, and for a year or more it involved Captain Berthoud very closely.

The enterprise was already in the planning stage when the Utah & Northern was still under survey, and during the late summer of 1878, Professor Joseph Luce of Berthoud's Golden office traced a highly provisional Georgetown Loop between Georgetown and Silver Plume, thereby becoming the first of at least four engineers to survey that dramatic passage. Hardly was the Montana expedition back in Colorado when the sturdy Tom Milner was again on reconnaissance, probing among the whitening peaks toward Leadville. On November 15, 1878, the telegraph from New York announced the incorporation of another Colorado Central subsidiary, the Georgetown, Leadville & San Juan. Loveland and Berthoud, by then in personal conference with Mr. Gould at 578 Fifth Avenue, obviously had much to do with it, and they even were listed as incorporators beside the names of Gould, Sidney Dillon, the president of the Union Pacific, and the extraordinary financier, Russell Sage. At the first regular meeting of the company, held at Golden on December 5, Loveland was elected president. Berthoud as usual became secretary and chief engineer.[23]

There was satisfaction in Golden — and another apotheosis of Loveland — but the local Colorado interests were once again doomed in frustration. The process was, as usual, polite but inexorable. Much of it was based upon the financial position of the Colorado Central vis a vis the Union Pacific; part of it was sweetened by freight rate adjustments that benefited Loveland and Golden at the expense of John Evans and Denver. But the Colorado Central remained a Union Pacific vassal, and its day-to-day affairs were managed from the east. New York and Boston controlled the substance. Golden retained, amid expensive mountain scenery, a Will o' the Wisp.[24]

The High Line did sponsor some extraordinary surveys. In March 1879, Berthoud's field party of twelve took the field. It presently grew to twenty-one, fed and directed from an enormous portable tent. Early in June his rodmen topped Bill Loveland's pass in bottomless slush, and by July 29 they had established a precise line up Ten Mile Canyon and through booming Leadville to a point on the Arkansas River below present-day Granite. Here they encountered the completed trackage of the competitive Denver & Rio Grande Railway, and their detailed determinations were abandoned in favor of a hasty reconnaissance. They crossed the Sawatch Range over hulking tundra via Cottonwood and Lake passes and located their line by triangulation through the continental divide by means of a 1.1-mile paper tunnel. On August 5, they completed their trek at Gunnison City, twenty-two miles short of the nearest San Juan Mountains and seven from the Ute Indian Reservation. Gunnison boasted fourteen houses; Berthoud pronounced it a "town in the future."[25]

Even this did not finish the season of 1879. There were supplementary examinations of Tennessee and Half Moon passes, plus tramps along the upper Eagle and lower Blue rivers. In addition, Berthoud was responsible for the usual special tasks, things like the preparation of reports and their presentation to senior management. Twice, on May 26 and September 26, he accompanied Gould aboard a specially fitted observation car from Golden to Georgetown, and he routinely kept in touch with the Union Pacific. In fact, the Union Pacific sent one of its principal engineers, Robert Blickensderfer, to Colorado to refine the alignment west of Georgetown, and in the autumn there emerged a perfected plan for the Georgetown Loop.[26]

In later years, it became customary to cite either Berthoud or Blickensderfer as the "Father of the Loop." Neither singularly deserves the honor; the two collaborated directly and in addition, the ground had been examined earlier by Luce and Milner. Moreover, it may be ventured that the Loop was not, in itself, a very great feat. It was a logical and picturesque response to some very awkward terrain, and its principal difficulty was less physical than financial. The Union Pacific executive committee viewed the proposal for many months with raised eyebrows, and the first regular passenger train did not pass over it until March 31, 1884.[27]

If the captain's performance as a "father" is seriously to be questioned, it is not with respect to his locations, but in the matter of his estimates. If Edward Berthoud suffered from a serious professional weakness, it was his tendency to under-calculate costs. His figures for the Utah & Northern are a fair example, but in the case of the Loop and the High Line he went overboard. Even assuming a narrow gauge and a stable dollar, his conclusions challenge belief. For a 3,500-foot tunnel beneath Loveland Pass he quoted $435,000; for a 1,400-foot bore at a higher level, $60,000; for the grading between the tunnel and Leadville, about fifty-one miles, $335,000; from the tunnel eastboud to Silver Plume, sixteen miles, $150,000; from Silver Plume to Georgetown, including the Loop, an incredibly low $45,000.[28] Actual costs for the eight-mile Georgetown to Graymont section would alone come to $245,000. Complex management was not his talent, and he often sought, perhaps unconsciously, to encourage enterprise by minimizing its price.

Nevertheless, technical underestimations were not the reason for Berthoud's departure from the High Line. As with the Colorado Central, his separation was gradual. He was retained as chief engineer as late as March 1881, and he did not relinquish his secretarial duties until the end of 1882. The crucial element was topographic. The route of the High Line was simply too forbidding for economical operation. As early as September 19, 1879, just as the captain was riding to

Georgetown with Gould aboard the latter's private car, it was rumored (correctly) that the financier was buying into the competing and partially completed Denver, South Park & Pacific. Gould that autumn was already adjusting his emphasis southward, ultimately to take in the Denver & Rio Grande and the Missouri Pacific. Polite appearances were, however, continued for a little longer. In February 1881, the Georgetown, Leadville & San Juan was reorganized as the Georgetown, Breckenridge & Leadville with only a partial rearrangement of its executive officers, and there even was some provisional grading along the face of Loveland Pass. But the company still was administered from the east, and Berthoud was presently relegated to the keeping of the minutes of the other men's decisions. His final resignation on December 4, 1882, was amicable. Gould and Dillon continued to think well of him and said so. Nevertheless, the High Line had by now been abandoned to summertime stage operations of the most primitive kind.[29]

The captain hardly yet realized that he had passed the peak of his railroad career. Bill Loveland's dreams for Golden died hard, and he characteristically sought substitutes for the High Line by way of alternative incorporations. One was called the Colorado Western. Organized in the spring of 1879, it produced extensive pencilings across the map, a pleasant exercise in which Bertoud participated, and it actually put Tom Milner and Edward Jones into the field. Another was the Golden, Georgetown and Central, a resuscitation of the earlier company that had sought to convert Berthoud's surveys of 1861 to railroad use. This time the captain became more deeply committed. From a temporary headquarters in Utah he observed the progress of an existing project called the Utah Southern and next re-examined his original Provo to Golden route, modifying his profiles wherever it seemed appropriate to do so. The changes were few. One reduced his Gore Pass gradient from 2.25 percent to 1.75 percent; another proposed a shorter tunnel beneath the crest of Berthoud Pass. This activity occupied most of the summer of 1880. Nothing came of it, and the surviving records, published and unpublished, are sparse.[30]

His subsequent undertakings were less ambitious. A hurried examination on April 17 and 18, 1880, of the terrain between Lyons and Estes Park helped to moderate a notorious wagon road, but Berthoud thought the route unsuitable for a railroad. In July 1881, he revisited Middle Park for reasons that are not entirely clear, but he reported a flurry of activity there (surveyors and graders of the South Park and Denver & Rio Grande companies), and he took hopeful note of the preliminaries on Loveland Pass. In the autumn of 1882, he probed the eastern San Juans in behalf of another scheme, the Del Norte, Summitville & Southwestern, and with the assistance of F.L. Dudley and Steven Higby (the latter had been with him in Montana) he labored across the stark uplands until dangerously late in the season. During the following summer he reappraised the whole region in greater detail.[31]

Little came of these efforts. Estes Park remained for many seasons unspoiled. The hustle in Middle Park quickly died away. Summitville (altitude 11,200 feet) entered an uncertain future without a railroad. And Berthoud himself would survey no further trackage, potential or actual, for a long time to come.

*   *   *

It is sometimes asserted that civil engineers are a precision-directed breed, engrossed in sines and cosines and by nature oblivious to the tastes and concerns of others. This is of course nonsense; slide rules can and do co-exist with essays and symphonies. It even is possible to identify an engineer as a "renaissance man," just as it is by no means unheard of to discover a renaissance man engaged in engineering. Moreover, there was much of the renaissance spirit in Edward L. Berthoud — his deficiencies in the matter of aesthetics notwithstanding.

The catholicity of his interests continued to the end of his life, and he seldom permitted the disciplines of the plane table to interfere with their pursuit. While employed in 1875 upon the Colorado Central near Georgetown, he found time for private rambles across the slopes of Mount McClellan, where he could examine alpine ice-caves and sub-alpine forests, and he noted, very astutely, that the upper limits of trees in Colorado coincided in terms of altitude with those in tropical latitudes. The Montana expedition of 1878 saw him at his perceptive best, and even the crash survey of the High Line in 1879 did not preclude a number of private investigations. He furthermore took care to publish his material. Mount McClellan appeared in the *American Journal of Science* in February 1876, and his data from 1878 was incorporated into a formal paper for the Davenport (Iowa) Academy of Natural Sciences, a now-forgotten but unusual body, whose president was a woman (Mrs. Mary L.D. Putnam) and whose membership included such luminaries as the botanist Charles Christopher Parry and the geologist Clarence King. His observations from the High Line were submitted to a regional, but fully accredited, journal called *The Kansas City Review of Science and Industry*. They featured a detailed commentary upon Colorado trees — species and biomes — in which Berthoud appears as an intelligent, if imperfect, amateur. He was strong on aspen and bristlecone pine, but turned uncertain over the douglasfir and, like many professionals then and since, bogged down among the willows.[32]

His activities in the eastern San Juans produced, in 1882, a particularly handsome extra dividend, an array of ancient rock art, incised in volcanic strata along a foothills canyon. There were, he noted, "all manner of pictures, symbols and hieroglyphics;" they were not paintings, and they differed considerably from certain aboriginal art that he earlier had examined in New Mexico. *The Kansas City Review* promptly published his findings, which were deemed so significant that they were quoted at length by the pioneer ethnologist Garrick Mallery. The site has since received repeated archaeological attention.[33]

Such extra-curricular investigations were often more than fortuitous. Early in 1881, the *Review* printed a well-thought-out article on the underground water resources of Colorado, presented in an impeccably scientific manner and featuring a shrewd assessment of the geologic structure of the southern Rockies. He turned also to history, especially the record of North American exploration, and by 1880, his personal library burgeoned with historical titles in several languages. He was especially attracted by oddities: the geographic notions of an obscure Italian mathematician (Antonio Magrino Petavino), an alleged Atlantic chart of Sebastian Cabot (1544), and the abundantly cited rescue of Horace Greeley from Clear Creek. Of special significance was another *Review* essay in which he suggested that the persistent notion of an insular California might have derived from a major spill of the Colorado River into the Salton Sink. "Captain Berthoud," declared George West in his *Transcript*, "is quite a historical society in himself."[34]

A number of these activities produced interesting acquaintances. One was Robert Orchard Old, an English promoter with a mixed

Edward L. Berthoud, one of Golden's first citizens, graying in middle age.
Courtesy of the Denver Public Library.

conscience, who pandered mines to the unsuspecting, but who also organized in London the British and Colorado Mining Bureau that collected, in part from Berthoud, a good deal of authentic information. During the 1870s, the captain contributed quantities of material to the Hayden Survey, both commentaries and specimens, to illustrate the regional geology of Colorado and the practical effects of its topography and climate. He consulted repeatedly with the brilliant young geologist and topographer Archibald Marvine, who adopted Berthoud's "mountain front" concepts almost intact, and he soon attracted the respect, not only of the pioneer geographer Henry Gannett, but of the grand old man of palaeobotany, Leo Lesquereux. "The authority of Captain Berthoud," declared Lesquereux, ". . . is considered as of great weight in geological matters in Colorado . . ." Berthoud took obvious satisfaction from brushing the sleeves of such giants, and it is a pity that he seems not to have encountered that most eminent of trios, Arnold Hague, geology, Clarence King, geology, and Henry Adams, who presently would dominate the whole sweep of American thought. Hague, King, and Adams visited Greeley and Estes Park in the mid-summer of 1871; alas, the captain was just then tramping the bottom of Clear Creek Canyon with the pleasant but intellectually undistinguished Frederick Dent Grant.[35]

By the early 1880s, Berthoud was well into his fifties. He was noticeably graying, but seemed only slightly less lithe than in his army days. He continued marvelously active, so much so that a number of his undertakings are difficult to place in context. He invented a "swinging" gunsight that progressed through a Washington patent attorney to a board of ordnance officers (which turned it down), and it eventually achieved an honorable interrment among the files of the French war office. He traded in real estate, briefly and without profit, at his boyhood home in Nelliston. He once again kept, temporarily, the weather records of Golden. He served, once or twice, as a statistician for Jefferson County. Thanks to his wife, he was kept reasonably current with good works and the social graces. Together they sponsored baptisms, supported the community opera house, and "received" their friends. Golden, though still outwardly stark, was by this time far from crude, and Helen Berthoud had had much to do with the process. One of her formal entertainments, on February 10, 1882, received detailed treatment in the Denver press.[36]

The unpaved streets of downtown Golden in the 1880s. *Courtesy of the Colorado Historical Society.*

But if he had an outside interest that dominated everything else it was the encouragement of education. Indeed, it bade fair to become his second profession.

He slipped into it naturally enough. Jefferson County abounded in common men, and common men are typically prone to hold the better educated in special awe. This is not, to be sure, always justified. Berthoud himself, as speaker of the Territorial House, had been a disaster, and the proper hours of a territorial librarian had hardly fitted the activities of a railroad surveyor. But as an occasional fountain of wisdom he was ideal, and we repeatedly find him on the Golden school board; in fact, he served as its president, beginning in 1874, for five uninterrupted years, and he acted as board secretary over most of the period between 1880 and 1892. Though certain of his colleagues proved less than competent, Golden sustained him cordially. Throughout he pressed quietly for a strengthened curriculum, in particular the preparation of the talented for entry into the recently organized Colorado

Students in front of Jarvis Hall, the Episcopal school which served as a predecessor of the Colorado School of Mines. This building burned in 1878. *Courtesy of the Colorado Historical Society.*

School of Mines.[37]

As a matter of fact it was the School of Mines that gave Berthoud his most effective opportunity for civic service. "Mines" had unusual roots. It initially developed from an educational enterprise of the Protestant Episcopal Church. As a church sponsored entity, however, it was the victim of an inordinate quantity of bad luck. Consecrated with a bishop's prayer in 1869, it had promptly been flattened by a foothills wind, and a decade later it burned to the ground. But between disasters it perched bravely upon the southerly fringes of Golden, and Berthoud, as the town's most accomplished Episcopal layman, had naturally much to do with it. Initially named Jarvis Hall, after a nationally known cleric, it sought to provide an all-male student body with an uncommonly sound regimen of classics, divinity, and natural science.[38]

But ill-luck is typically costly, and even before it opened its doors

Jarvis found itself in such financial distress that its trustees were driven to seek government support. The territorial assembly (it now met exclusively in Denver) proved surprisingly sympathetic. Coached by Messrs. Welch, West, and Berthoud, it neatly side-stepped any legal difficulties over an appropriation for a religious institution on February 10, 1870, by making a grant to a "School of Mines," which in reality encompassed the scientific portion of the Jarvis curriculum. This for the moment sufficed. The tempest-tossed litter of the original school was quickly reassembled, and a taxpayer-subsidized technical school found itself ensconced within an ecclesiastical cocoon. It had been rather obviously Berthoud-crafted, and he even served, albeit errati-cally, upon its faculty, lecturing to students and townspeople upon geology and engineering and their special applications to the extraction of minerals. [39]

Yet it was never a stable arrangement. From the start there was an embarrassing uncertainty over administrative responsibilities. Berthoud was happy enough in his occasional duties, and he even acted during the first academic year (1870-1871) as a "Professor of Botany," the first such appointment in Colorado. (Contemporary notices also indicate that he held an A.M. degree, the details of which escape us.) But he eventually became disillusioned with the Jarvis-Mines connection, and within four years he joined with West, Welch, and Loveland to petition for its dissolution. Again the legislature obliged, and on February 9, 1874, it directed that the "School of Mines" be placed under the exclusive jurisdiction of the territorial government; furthermore, it sweetened the rearrangement with an additional allocation of $5,000. Less than five months later, the first specifically "Mines" board of trustees met in Golden. They might as well have been the board of the Colorado Central — W.A.H. Loveland was chosen president and E.L. Berthoud secretary. And in September there appeared the first formal "Mines" catalog, drafted by Berthoud and printed by George West's *Transcript*. [40]

Formal independence inspired several contributions of land (the captain himself was a donor), yet the actual separation from Jarvis was painfully slow. For three additional years Loveland and Berthoud could claim no functioning school over which to preside, and when someone suggested that Mines should prepare an exhibit for the 1876 Centennial Exposition at Philadelphia, the captain was obliged to assemble it

The Colorado School of Mines as Berthoud knew it. *Courtesy of the Denver Public Library.*

himself. (It did receive a bronze medal.) The first formal School of Mines diploma was not awarded until 1883, and there were times when Berthoud simply threw up his hands in despair. Yet Mines survived as a notion and at last as a fact, and by 1880 it was established in its own building. Berthoud with understandable pride pronounced it "an ornament to the town and a credit to the state."[41]

Yet he remained primarily a civil engineer, and with his profession he continued involved with a variety of projects. If Colorado offered exhilarating space and superb scenery, it suffered from a fundamental lack of rainfall, and the first concern of its inhabitants has been — always — the collection and distribution of water. It was of course inevitable that Berthoud should be caught up in the process. An early example was the Vasquez Flume and Ditch Company. Organized in 1870, it was a quasi-public undertaking, with a board of trustees that embraced much of the executive talent of Jefferson County. Berthoud, one suspects, administered less than he labored, calculating flow, placing headgates, and perfecting alignments. But though the Vasquez was a considerable enterprise, its initial fortunes were mixed. The captain had endorsed several of its notes, and in October 1876, a financial crisis required a "settlement" that cost him $400 and fully satisfied no one. A later project in the mid-1880s was the Golden Ditch and Flume Company, which sought to divert water from behind the hogbacks at Glencoe, five miles above Golden. It even comprehended a narrow gauge railway, the "Denver & Middle Park," for the exploitation of local building stone. The ditches and flumes were elaborate, and they occupied months of Berthoud's time. They handsomely fulfilled their intended purpose and, in modified form, still do. The railway, however, lost money lavishly, was palmed off on the Union Pacific, and eventually, in 1898, was abandoned.[42]

For a long period Berthoud had comparatively little to do with conventional public highways. He did serve from 1875 to 1878 as Jefferson County surveyor, and in 1885, he acted as advisor to an extensive county road expansion. His other undertakings led to a scattering of special ventures, none of them very profitable; a sampling works at Black Hawk and a mine in Chaffee County are representative. Like almost everyone in Golden, he juggled with city lots, again without conspicuous success, and he once was cited, in the spring of 1876, as a major tax delinquent. Among his ledgers we further learn that three of his nieces, Kate, Emily, and Eva, had come to reside in Golden, sometimes in his own household, and that he presented them with gifts of real estate on the occasion of their marriages. Emily and Eva were daughters of his brother Alexander. Kate poses an enigma. Originally a Ferrell, she subsequently assumed the Berthoud name, but there is no formal evidence of an adoption.[43]

His private activities continued multifarious. Following the weddings of the nieces, he and Helen appear to have taken in boarders, and there were occasional clusters of household servants, both black and white. In association with one Bellam he again served as the local agent of several old-line insurance companies, and along with policies and claims came two terms of service as a notary public. In company with his wife, he managed a number of veterans' reunions, and at one of these, on February 8, 1877, he presented an extensive and still very useful history of the Second Colorado Regiment. He was a frequent visitor at the two local newspapers, of which he openly preferred

George West's *Transcript*; it was, he was happy to stress, "Democratic from top to bottom, from keel to maintop." The Republican *Globe* he damned with faint praise: "It is a creditable sheet — technically speaking." As a natural recruit for boards and committees, he sometimes over-extended himself, and on one occasion in 1883 he rather shamefully neglected a Jefferson County exhibit intended for a state exposition in Denver. But Helen supplemented him to perfection; she literally feasted upon "obligation," filling the house with eastern visitors, conducting informal little scenic tours, and criss-crossing Golden and, indeed, much of the state, with cheerful visits to the unfortunate.[44]

Then came tragedy. On the evening of Friday, July 29, 1887, quite without warning, Helen Berthoud collapsed at her home with an acute stroke of apoplexy. She lapsed swiftly into unconsciousness, and it soon became evident that nothing could be done to save her. There was a melancholy period of waiting, but the end came quickly enough. "Dear Helen," wrote Berthoud in his old French Bible, "died August 2nd 1887 at 8:40 a.m. Loved forever 'we hope to meet again.' "

Her passing shocked the entire region. In Denver, the three principal newspapers published unabashed eulogies, but the response of Golden surpassed belief. Helen's funeral was conducted from Calvary Church at 10:00 a.m., Wednesday, August 4, and on that morning not a single local business establishment remained open. So deeply had this community come to love their little captain's lady.[45]

CHAPTER VI

The Final Decades

Without Helen, life would never be the same. A special graciousness had gone out of it.

For a year or more the little captain lived alone in his old residence as the corner of First (now Twelfth) Avenue and Washington Street. It by now was softened by the shade of poplar and pear trees, for Golden at last was undergoing a greening. Yet the place did not really suit his needs. He had never been conventionally gregarious. His preferred social contacts were limited, and never for an instant did he consider a second marriage. Eventually, therefore, he moved his effects — apparatus, curiosities, and books — to lesser accommodations on the second floor of the old Overland Hotel, directly above his existing offices and immediately to the south of George West's *Transcript*. The overflow of his collections he donated to the recently organized county historical society.[1]

Some began to think him eccentric, which is not an uncommon fate for an unusual man. It is probable that his new lodgings quickly degenerated into a dusty warren, and it is certain that Golden became bemused with certain of his habits. He was never an authentic recluse; he frequently sponsored high repartee amid the litter of his rooms, and his reputation as a scholar continued undiminished. His public demeanor was typically courtly, but he was conspicuously shy with women; he abhorred conventional hat-doffings and resorted instead to a curiously restrained salute. He was not slow, on the other hand, to evince his dissatisfactions, and he repeatedly discouraged over-

Edward L. Berthoud in his later years. *Courtesy of the Colorado Historical Society.*

lengthy Sunday sermons by unlimbering a huge pocket watch and winding it conspicuously. He was never truly seedy, and for years he conducted a remarkably successful opposition to the effects — physical and mental — of advancing age.[2]

As an acknowledged sage, he contributed numerous letters to editors, most frequently to George West of the *Transcript*, and when sometimes they failed to appear there would be "words." In 1889, he unleashed a diatribe against the late General John A. Logan, the classic veterans' politician and creator of Memorial Day; this set off a positive furor, and Berthoud subsequently was denied his usual office in the local chapter of the Grand Army of the Republic.[3]

Writing, in fact, was an effective therapy for the loss of Helen and it was by no means confined to opinions in the press. He soon turned to his monographs, both scientific and historical. Some were of indifferent quality; a treatise upon the Natchez Indians exhibited a deficient knowledge of the sources and a less-than-brilliant evaluation of the premises. But another, a brief but comprehensive dissertation upon the birds of Colorado, still deserves attention. It attempted, with considerable success, to explain avian paleontology, and it was distinctly perceptive as to ecological relationships. Like many amateurs, Berthoud stressed his rarities, and there was an inevitable resurrection of the Carolina parakeet and the white-winged dove. Yet he remained a careful observer; his doves and parrots were probably authentic stragglers, while his bobolinks, woodcocks, and scarlet tanagers survive to this day as certified casuals on the Colorado list. When, in 1898, he presented his records to W.W. Cooke, the first professional ornithologist at the State Agricultural Experiment Station, they were seriously received.[4]

There were times when Berthoud seemed an even better botanist than birder. In 1890, he introduced the promising young naturalist, Ellsworth Bethel, to the edible plants of the Western Slope, in particular the Yampa root, long esteemed by the Utes. Two years later the magisterial *Botanical Gazette* published his comments upon the extraordinary proliferation of certain plains flora, especially the sand plum and the *Rhus glabra*, a phenomenon that he ascribed (probably correctly) to the migratory bison. But in a later and very different essay he was less successful. Entitled *The Ice Age and Pliocene Man*, it neglected the botanical and advanced the curious notion that the earth's

The Overland Hotel in Golden, where Berthoud spent his later years, seen here in demolition. *Courtesy of the Colorado Historical Society.*

rotation, world glaciation, and the appearance of man were essentially simultaneous events of the Pliocene, and it furthermore noted, by way of confirmation, that Holy Scripture treated light, darkness, and humanity as nearly coincident. It was not his most impressive effort, and it was distributed at his own expense.[5]

His historical contributions were usually more credible. They began as occasional chores for others — translations from French for the Colorado historian, Frank Hall, and a search, for an inquirer in Louisiana, among the records of a Swiss mercenary regiment stationed on the Gulf coast during the Seven Years War. In his final years he resumed his interest in the earlier French penetrations of the Far West, but his first significant historical publication was an inquiry into the location of Francis Drake's anchorage in California. This appeared in an early issue of the *National Geographic*, on December 29, 1894, which was not even then a journal of a strictly scholarly character, but Berthoud did consult the more obvious authorities, and it is clear that he contributed some thinking of his own. He chose, as Drake's probable landing place, Bodega Bay, which was not far, in terms of locale and configuration, from the site, Drake's Bay, that is nowadays accepted. Moreover, he declared without qualification that Drake must have been unaware of the Bay of San Francisco, an opinion that has since become orthodox.[6]

Although his Franco-American studies have not always been confirmed by subsequent scholarship, they do deserve examination. In another private pamphlet, which appeared in 1897, he advanced the unusual thesis that the French regarded ancient Louisiana as a transcontinental tract, stretching, northward of the Forty-Second Parallel, unbroken to the Pacific. In support of this, he cited de Lusson's pow-wow at Sault Ste. Marie in 1671, the mid-continental probings of the La Vérendryes, and selected clauses from the secret Franco-Spanish agreement of 1800. He also could point to the subsequent presence of Lewis and Clark at the mouth of the Columbia. But when he dismissed the British claims to Oregon as "trumped up," he flew in the face of facts. Americans, however, applauded his position, and his essay was reprinted in Gulf Magazine in 1902 and listed in the highly respectable Writings on American History in 1904.[7]

Even more interesting was an undated manuscript upon the La Vérendrye Expedition of 1742-1743, in which Berthoud suggested that the party had reached the Wasatch Mountains (though not the Great Salt Lake) and had returned to the Missouri River by way of the Platte. It was a semi-scholarly presentation of twenty-three pages, based upon La Vérendrye's published journal and the later comments of Margry, Garneau, and the Abbé Duges; in addition, Berthoud obviously drew upon his own extensive personal knowledge of the terrain. The text was accompanied by a carefully executed map, forty miles to the inch, indicating likely compass headings and rates of travel. Although this particular study never saw print, it was evidently intended for publication, and it was circulated rather widely among interested readers.[8]

Berthoud eventually came to be recognized as a serious authority on France in the American West. Although his name was hardly a byword upon the more prestigious campuses, he did work frequently with organizations like the Quivera Historical Society (an "Association of Explorers, Authors and Ethnologic Students," with headquarters in Alma, Kansas) and with the recently founded Historical Society of

New Mexico in Santa Fe. In 1903, he received a formal invitation from the State of Louisiana to take part in the centennial celebrations of the famous Purchase, and though he appears not to have attended, he continued to serve as a one-man information bureau for the history of the entire region. His most frequent correspondent was a bright young Kansan named George J. Remsburg, for whom he burned much midnight oil, and his upstairs lodgings became a major repository of superceded maps, out-of-print journals, and dog-eared reports.[9]

His civic activities continued spasmodic. His secretarial services still were sought by the Opera House Company, the board of which often met in his office. He furthermore served a term, from April 1890 to April 1891, as mayor of Golden. He accepted the latter position with reluctance, but the sole regular nominee, R.C. Wells, had found it necessary to withdraw, and both the captain and the community probably thought it suitable that a "Mayor Berthoud" should appear somewhere in the record.[10]

In any case, it was a quiet administration. His Honor "had the calaboose rejuvenated somewhat," listened to criticisms of the muddy streets (wherein the cattle still roamed), and worried appropriately over aging bridges. Golden, in truth, was stagnant. The up-canyon mines marked time; the basic contest with Denver had long since been lost. Only the brewery of Adolph Coors contributed a hopeful pungency to the local atmosphere.[11]

The captain's association with Calvary Church continued unbroken. The little parish probably did not fulfill every expectation of its founders, and the $60 (total) that was placed in offering on Sunday, January 26, 1890, was thought so extraordinary that George West took public notice of it in his newspaper. Yet Calvary continued its mission without substantial crisis, and Berthoud continued steadily upon its vestry. His Sunday attendance was as faithful as a civil engineer could make it, and he became, at marriages and baptisms, a recognized father-figure. That he never received formal Episcopal confirmation remains a matter for astonishment.[12]

But his primary civic concern remained the School of Mines, for here was the cause that best fitted his talents. His formal ties with the institution were sometimes broken; after 1881, he departed from the faculty for good, and for an entire decade, from 1889 to 1899, he did not sit on the board. But there was a continuing relationship;

Calvary Church in Golden, which Berthoud served so long, but never formally joined. *Courtesy of the Denver Public Library.*

survey work, a building committee, and, in the mid-1890s, an on-campus supervision of weather records. The last was vintage Berthoud, with extensive supplementary data as to blossomings, frogs, garter snakes, and, on March 18, 1895, an eclipse of the moon. Finally, in the winter of 1899, a nomination by Governor Charles S. Thomas, a Democrat, put him back on the board.[13]

Berthoud obviously was pleased. We read of a gift to the school of a "number of valuable works;" moreover, this latest period of service would continue well into 1903 and would involve an interesting, indeed critical, period in the institution's development. Mines completed the old century with 244 students, not all of whom were amenable to the no-nonsense standards imposed by the current president, Charles S. Palmer. In February 1900, the entire freshman class walked out in protest over the rigor of their assignments, but neither administration nor trustees flinched, and those students who ultimately chose to return were obligated to re-register. Nonetheless, when Palmer expanded his reforms to include an evaluation of the whole faculty, a state of panic gripped the school and affected even the board.[14]

The board's current chairman was the well-known king of Cripple Creek, Winfield Scott Stratton, who held the post for the usual reason — the expectation (handsomely fulfilled) of gifts. But Stratton had come from a plain background and could muster only a moderate commitment to rigid academic standards. Berthoud's viewpoint was naturally quite different, and he could not in good conscience oppose an improvement in the quality of the professorate. Yet he too had experienced much of the workaday world and understood the appeal of a more practical element in the curriculum. He therefore proposed that Mines should offer an alternative two-year program for the training of foremen. It was probably unfortunate that his suggestion, though carefully considered, was not adopted.[15]

Stratton died in 1902, and in 1903 the whole school erupted. At their April meeting, the trustees were bluntly told that the entire faculty would resign unless Palmer was dismissed. The immediate response of the board is unknown, but the impasse was resolved a few days later by the resignation of *both* president and faculty, an arrangement that opened the way for a new administration which could replace, or re-appoint, at its pleasure.[16]

Berthoud departed with Palmer, but in no way under a cloud. He

Berthoud Hall, Colorado School of Mines, as it looked in the 1980s. *Courtesy of Robert C. Black, III.*

concluded his service with the sincere good wishes of his colleagues and an honorary degree as Engineer of Mines. Whether it was bestowed at his last commencement is uncertain; the Mines alumni office now-adays believes that it was, but the contemporary local press made no mention of it. We nevertheless can be certain that Edward L. Berthoud retired from his beloved school as a respected alumnus.[17]

But his supreme loyalty would always be to his profession. The absence of elaborate retirement programs was one reason; professional activity produced an income. Yet this was hardly his principal motive. As a lonely widower he simply could not conceive of life without it. Only an unexpected misfortune would prevent him from literally dying in harness.

Though his commissions continued frequent enough, they were seldom of the pioneering kind; primary traverses of the wilderness were by the century's turn few and far between. Instead, he found himself engrossed in routine chores — homely things like the perfection of irrigation systems and the improvement of existing roads and bridges, tasks of necessity, yet little noted, then or now.

There was, however, one extensive new project, an interurban railroad between Denver and Golden, the kind of light, flexible carrier that the 1890s thought useful as a supplementary connection between existing communities. Undertakings of this sort were typically electrified and were generally, though not exclusively, intended for passenger traffic; furthermore, they often operated upon or beside existing roads and streets. When completed, Berthoud's interurban was named the Denver, Lakewood & Golden.

This enterprise was first seriously considered as early as 1887, when the captain ran a tentative reconnaissance over the whole projected route, but there was no formal incorporation until July 1890, and his detailed survey (374 stations, with summaries of excavation, masonry, and timber work) required several additional months. His alignment ran westward through pastures and farms straight as a ruling grade of 2 percent would permit, to South Table Mountain and thence around its southerly and westerly perimeters into Golden. There was in addition a short-lived branch from Golden northward toward the coal fields of Ralston Creek. A franchise for the use of Golden's streets was approved at a simple citizen's rally, nor was the fact that Berthoud was currently mayor regarded as a conflict of interest. Operations, complete with electrification, were confidently expected for December, but there were difficulties, chiefly financial, and the first passenger train did not reach Golden from Denver until September 20, 1891 — behind steam power. Electrification and a reasonably stable financial structure did not come for eighteen more years.[18]

His other activities are recorded chiefly in his notebooks. For Jefferson County there was a highway along the township line between 3 and 4 South, Range 69 West (1888) and a county boundary road across the valley of Clear Creek (1889). Also in 1889, we encounter a preliminary Glencoe Dam, plus an experimental resort community, centered on Lookout Mountain and dedicated to the summertime comfort of Denver businessmen; for the latter, he completed 16.70 miles of meets and bounds. In 1890, he conducted extensive work for the Welch Main Ditch, the Welch Lateral Ditch, the Kountz and Downing Ditch, the Wyman Reservoir, and, for the famous old militiaman Major Jacob Downing, a one-half mile race course. His most rigorous assignment came in July 1899, when he ran an irrigation reconnaissance from an elevated point on South Boulder Creek, 500 feet above the present Moffat Tunnel, thence southeasterly on a 2 percent grade to an ascertained level of 7,326.05 feet on Ralston Creek. The survey traversed consistently difficult country and terminated in a sharply incised canyon. "The Epitomy of Cussedness," wrote Berthoud's levelman, A.K. Townsend; "the damdest place ever set up in." "Amen," added the captain. He was by this time seventy-one years of age.[19]

He completed his eighth decade without apparent degeneration. His later photographs do reveal snowy-white hair and partial baldness, and his figure had turned a little less lithe. But his vigor remained such that his friends ceased to remark upon it; it was simply assumed. He quite eschewed conventional relaxation, but he held constant discourse, both oral and by correspondence, upon an enormous range of topics, and he kept in frequent touch, in French, with an array of European relatives. He maintained his scholarly memberships, continued to serve as a notary public, and underwrote a considerable volume of insurance policies, both fire and life. On March 29, 1908, he attained his eightieth birthday, still capable of a full day's work in the field, and he in fact celebrated the event by running the lines of a forty-acre tract.[20]

It was however, his last professional effort. On the evening of April 7, he lit a kerosene lamp and was ascending the stairs to his bedroom when he was seized with a sudden dizziness and tumbled helplessly down the entire flight to the floor below. There he lay bleeding and senseless, while the smashed lamp sent rivulets of flame across the planking. The fire, very fortunately, attracted immediate attention; the front door was forced and the flames extinguished, while the unconscious Berthoud was placed upon a makeshift bed in his office. A physician, Dr. John P. Kelly, was summoned and found that the captain's injuries were not of themselves critical. There were cuts on his head, face, and arms and some very extensive bruises, but no broken bones. Moreover, the patient promptly regained consciousness and peremptorily forbade any special nursing care for the remainder of the night.[21]

Many, including Berthoud himself, thought it had been no more than a nasty accident and that a complete and early recovery would follow. He withstood in courageous style a brutal little operation for the removal of part of his nose, and on the afternoon of April 10, he received in good-natured audience an enterprising young reporter named Louis Meyer from the *Denver Times*. He promised Mr. Meyer that he would write an account of his life as soon as his arms were free from bandages and observed that "a little more or less nose won't make much difference to a man of my age." Already he had resumed his insurance business with the help of an assistant.[22]

But there remained the hidden effects of shock — and the question of his original dizziness. He was in fact advised to keep to his bed, and it was sometime later when, in defiance of instructions, he ventured alone into his kitchen that he suffered a second fall. Thereafter he failed rapidly and late in May was carried to the house of nearby friends, Mr. and Mrs. J.H. Brown, and placed under the care of a trained nurse. There on the afternoon of June 13, 1908, he quietly died.[23]

No special cause of death was cited at the time, other than "injuries from a fall."[24] Yet one may suggest, on grounds of subsequent medical knowledge, a series of strokes. In any case, it is pleasant to know that he was obliged to suffer so brief a period of helplessness.

His passing was appropriately noted, although not with the spontaneity of Helen's. The *Transcript* was most emotional — "Pathfinder crosses Range to Eternal City beyond" — and published a recent photograph in a frame of spruce trees. Somewhat unexpectedly, the *Denver Republican* ran a eulogistic lead editorial, citing the debt owed him by younger generations of Coloradoans (it did, however, ignore his Democratic proclivities). Most curious of all was the response of the *Denver Times*, which chose, despite young Meyer, not to mention his death at all.[25]

His funeral was briefly delayed for an astonishing reason. Someone had retrieved a memorandum from among his effects, asking that his body be held a day or two longer than customary in order to prevent any possibility of his being buried alive, and someone else promptly recalled that he had expressed this concern for some time. The services were eventually held at the Brown residence on June 16; they were performed by Calvary's rector, the Reverend Mr. Pullen, in accordance with the rites of the church that Berthoud had served for so long, but had never formally joined. Few of his old associates were present; most, indeed, were dead. George West had passed away in November of

1906. Charles Welch had died the previous February. Bill Loveland had rested, since 1894, beneath the sod of victorious Denver. Silas Burt still lived, but his ties with Berthoud had long since faded quietly away. Best known among the mourners were Regis Chauvenet and Judge Moses Hallett, men who had known and respected him as a fellow faculty and board member at the School of Mines.[26]

He was buried beside Helen in Golden Cemetery, in a bare little plot as yet unbeautified. His marker was minimal; a more suitable monument awaited the generosity of others, especially of Golden's famous brewer, Adolph Coors. The captain's estate was far from handsome; it was, thanks to a legal defect, merely intricate. Its liquid assets came to less than $2,000, and it was presently learned that he had for some time contributed much of his income to the support of an elder sister, Matilda, an obscure expatriate artist of advanced senility. His principal books and papers did find ultimate and suitable resting places, but his private effects, the personal letters and family photographs, were strewn beyond practicable recall among nephews and nieces from Massachusetts to California, and to this extent our ability to estimate the captain and his lady has been distinctly impaired.[27]

Nevertheless, a final critique may be ventured. It need not be lengthy or contrived.

Edward Louis Berthoud once was cited as "the greatest figure in Colorado's colorful history."[28] This, on its face, is a large exaggeration. Berthoud was a *secondary* figure — seldom a chairman, typically a secretary, commonly employed (albeit in an exacting profession) by others — the eternal subordinate. Yet who will say that he does not deserve his pass, his town, and his hall?

For Berthoud, quite simply, was not an ordinary person. If he was typically of secondary rank, he was *useful* beyond most of his contemporaries. In a milieu that demanded the practical, he supplied high technical competence. At a time and place too frequently marred by extremists, he proffered (with a whimsical exception or two) moderation. In the wilderness, he remained civilized.

Least ordinary of all was the exceptional time-span of his contributions. They may never have attracted universal attention, but they ran unbroken with the national destiny through six of the most critical decades of American history.

E N D N O T E S

ABBREVIATIONS OF FREQUENTLY USED CITATIONS

BLM — Bureau of Land Management.
BP — E.L. Berthoud Papers, Colorado Historical Society.
CSA — Colorado State Archives.
CHS — Colorado Historical Society.
CM — *Colorado Magazine*
CSM — Colorado School of Mines.
DAB — *Dictionary of American Biography.*
DPL — Denver Public Library.
DPLW — Denver Public Library, Western History Department.
ELB — Edward L. Berthoud.
GCT — *Golden Colorado Transcript.*
GG — *Golden Globe.*
KCRS — *Kansas City Review of Science and Industry.*
KHQ — *Kansas Historical Quarterly.*
KSHS — Kansas State Historical Society.
NCAB — *National Cyclopaedia of American Biography.*
NYPL — New York Public Library.
ORA — *Official Records of Union and Confederate Armies.*
RMN — *Rocky Mountain News.*

127

ENDNOTES — CHAPTER I

1. Oral statement, John R. Berthoud, September 18, 1978; Telephone Directory, *Denver and the Greater Metro Area* (1979).

2. Genealogical materials, John R. Berthoud Collection, West Hartford, Conn.; J.-B. Riepstap and V. and H.V. Rolland, comps., *Illustrations to the Armorial General* (2 vols., Baltimore, 1967) I, Plate CXCVI; J.-B. Riepstap, comp., *The Armorial General* (2 vols., Baltimore, 1965) II, 1200 (supplement); Karl Baedeker *et al.*, comps., *Switzerland* (Leipzig, London, and New York, 1913), 24. A special collection of Berthoud vital statistics lies among the municipal records of Switzerland.

3. Notes in ELB's hand on flyleaf of Berthoud family's *La Sainte Bible*, Colorado Historical Society (hereafter cited as CHS); transcript in Genealogical Division, Denver Public Library (hereafter cited as DPL); statement of Byron Nellis in Ruth V. Lupo, *Waymarks of Nelliston, N.Y.* (Fort Plain, N.Y., 1978), 45; U.S. Census, 1850, Town of Palatine, N.Y.

4. ELB birth certificate, City of Geneva, Photocopy in L.D.S. Family Library, Salt Lake City; ELB notes, *La Sainte Bible,*, n. 3; also gravestone of Frederic Stephen Berthoud, Ft. Plain, N.Y. For Margaret Berthoud see U.S. Census of 1850 (Town of Palatine, N.Y.).

5. No Berthouds were recorded in New York City in the first half of 1830; but two (Charles Louis and Nicolas) were listed as merchants in the city as of the beginning of 1831. U.S. Census Index, New York, 1830; Thos. Longworth, comp., *Longworth's . . . New York City Directory* (1830-31), 127; (1831-32), 129. No Berthoud arrivals are indicated in the surviving ships' passenger lists for these years.

6. *Longworth's Directory* (1830-31 through 1841-42); Simon De Witt, publ., *Map of the City and County of New York* (1832); Cholera Centers Map (untitled) of New York City (1832), N.Y. Public Library.

7. Statement of Byron Nellis in Lupo, *Waymarks*, 45.

8. N.Y. State Census 1855, Town of Palatine, N.Y.; letter, Peter Dey to Grenville Dodge, quoted in J.R. Perkins, *Trails, Rails and War: The Life of General G. M. Dodge* (Indianapolis, 1928), 123-124.

9. For such variations in spelling of names, cf. ELB's notations in *La Sainte Bible*; Last Will and Testament, Charles Henry Louis Berthoud; U.S. Census of 1850, Palatine, N.Y.; *1869-70 Business Directory, Montgomery and Fulton Counties, N.Y.*

10. *Longworth's Directory* (1831-2), 85, 129; De Witt, *Map of New York*, n. 6.

11. *Longworth's Directory* (1831-32), 129; (1832-33), 144; (1833-34), 122; (1835-36), 93; (1839-40), 96; (1842-43), 42-3, 90; *Doggett's New York City Directory* (1842-43), 32; (1843-44), 35; (1844-45), 37; (1845-46), 38.

12. Lupo, *Waymarks*, 43, 45; Book of Deeds No. 32, p. 116, Montgomery County Courthouse, Fonda, N.Y.; Cholera Centers Map, n. 6.

13. Book of Deeds, n. 12.

14. U.S. Census, Palatine, N.Y., 1850; Lupo, *Waymarks*, 45; Will of "Charles H." Berthoud, June 17, 1874, Surrogate's Court, Montgomery County, Fonda, N.Y.; Book of Deeds No. 36, p. 91, Montgomery County Courthouse, Fonda, N.Y.; Lupo, *Waymarks*, 46-7; Alvin F. Harlow, *The Road of the Century* (New York, 1947), 31, 271; Ruth V. Lupo to author, Feb. 15, 1979.

15. Lupo, *Waymarks*, 36-7, 42-4, 64; Harlow, *Road*, 27, 31; John F. Stover *Iron Road to the West* (Chicago, 1978), 163, 171.

16. Lupo, *Waymarks*, 147; Nelson Greene, *The Story of Old Fort Plain* (Ft. Plain, N.Y., 1947), 296; Silas Wright Burt, "My Personal Reminiscenses" (ms. in 4 vols., Mss. Division, New York Historical Society) III, 123; ms. Index, The Reformed Church, Fort Plain, Dept. of History and Archives, Montgomery County, Fonda, N.Y.

17. Reminiscenses of Oscar Geetz, cited in Charles S. Ryland, ". . . Berthoud," *Denver Westerners Monthly Roundup* XXI, No. 9, p. 9; Louis Mayer in Denver *Times*, April 11, 1908; E.L. Berthoud photographs in CHS and Western History Dept., DPL.

18. J. Colin James, Jr., "Captain Edward Louis Berthoud . . . ," *Purple and Gold* LX, No. 2, 89.

19. Andrew Van Vranken Raymond, *Union University* . . . (3 vols., New York, 1907) III, 120, 124 *et seq.*; Burt, Reminiscences I, 143; Thomas C. Reeves, *Gentleman Boss: The Life of Chester Alan Arthur* (New York, 1975), 8; Union College, *Union (Catalogue for 1979-1980)* (Schenectady, N.Y., 1979), 8. For a brief sketch of Silas Burt, see Edward A. Collier, *A History of Old Kinderhook* (New York and London, 1914), 45-47.

20. *Union* (Catalogue n. 19), 11-12; *National Cyclopaedia of American Biography* (hereafter cited as NCAB) VII, 170-71.

21. *Union* (Catalogue), 8-9; Codman Hislop, *Eliphalet Nott* (Middletown, Conn., 1971), 435-54; Eliphalet Nott, letter of introduction for ELB, Jan. 8, 1849, ELB Papers, Colorado Historical Society (hereafter cited as BP); Reeves, *Gentleman Boss*, 8.

22. Raymond, *Union* I, 216-20; Burt, "Reminiscenses" I, 150-1; Frederick W. Seward, *Reminiscenses of a War-Time Statesman* . . . (New York, 1916), 61-2, 65-6; Ruth V. Lupo to author, Feb. 15, 1979.

23. Burt, "Reminiscences" I, 150-1; Seward, *Reminiscences*, 66.

24. Cooper to Scott, Jan. 3, 1849, *Colorado Magazine* (hereafter cited as CM) VIII, 79, also original and photostat in BP; letter of Eliphalet Nott, Jan. 8, 1849, BP; Beard, ed., *Letters and Journals of James Fenimore Cooper* V, 395 and notes.

25. Testimonial letter, W.H. Talcott, dated April 26, 1852, BP; Carter Goodrich *et al.*, *Canals and American Economic Development* (New York & London, 1961), 146-7; Henry Sinclair Drago, *Canal Days in America* . . . (New York, 1972), 119-21; sketch of Talcott, NCAB IX, 43.

26. Contract, ELB and Panama R.R. Co., April 21, 1851, BP.

27. Thomas Harrison, delin., *Isthmus of Panama 1855. Map and Profile of the Panama Railroad* . . . (Kingston, Jamaica, 1855, copy in NYPL); *Panama Canal Review* (Jan. 28, 1955), 3.

28. ELB Letters, *Trail* XIII, No. 11, p. 11, and *The Sister Republics* (Nov., 1904), 6; F.N. Otis, *Illustrated History of the Panama Railroad* (reprint, Pasadena, Calif., 1971), 31-3; Joseph L. Schott, *Rails across Panama* . . . (Indianapolis, New York & Kansas City, 1867), 80-3.

29. *Trail* III, No. 11, p. 11; NCAB XVIII, 109-10; Schott, *op. cit.*, 81-3; ELB, *Birds: Their Geological History, Migration and Uses* (Golden, Colo., 1887 — pamplet), 17. (The range of the American Woodcock does not extend south of the co-terminous U.S.)

30. Alexander Saunders, "Short History of the Panama Railroad," *Bulletin*, Ry. & Loco. Hist. Soc., No. 78 (Oct. 1949), 13-4; Otis, *Panama R.R.*, 33; *Trail* XIII, No. 11, p. 11; ELB in *The Sister Republics* (Nov. 1904), 6; John Haskell Kemble, *The Panama Route, 1848-1869* (Berkeley & Los Angeles, 1943), 185-6.

31. ELB letter in *The Sister Republics* (Nov., 1904), 6.

32. Schott, *Rails across Panama*, 115, 139; ELB in *The Sister Republics* (Nov., 1904), 6; Saunders, *Short History*, 14-5; Lloyd Lewis, *Captain Sam Grant* (Boston, 1950), 299-307; Ulysses S. Grant, *Personal Memoirs of U.S. Grant* (2nd ed., 2 vols., New York, 1895), 156; John Y. Simon, ed., *Papers of U.S. Grant* (5 vols., Carbondale, Ill., 1967-1973) I, 252, 261, 482.

33. Contract, ELB and Panama R.R., April 21, 1851, BP; *Trail* XIII, No. 11, p. 11; ELB in *The Sister Republics* (Nov. 1904), 6.

34. Lupo, *Waymarks*, 148; Book of Deeds No. 68, p. 529, Montgomery County Courthouse, Fonda, N.Y.; Lupo to author, Feb. 15, 1979.

35. Wallace B. Turner, "Kentucky in a Decade of Change, 1850-1860" (typed Ph.D. dissertation, University of Ky., 1954), 178-9; Preserved Smith, "Neil Macneale, Railroad Builder of the Middle West, 1826-1897," *Mississippi Valley Historical Review* XXVI, 181-92; E.G. Sulzer, "A Kentucky Thoroughbred . . . ", *Bulletin No. 102*, Ry. & Loco. Hist. Soc. (Apr. 1960), 6-7.

36. Burt, "Reminiscences" II, 52-3; Preserved Smith, note 37.

37. U.S. Geological Survey sheet, *Maysville West, Ky.-Ohio*, 1961; Yoseloff, reprinter, *Official Atlas of the Civil War* (New York & London, 1958), plate CXLI.

38. Burt, "Reminiscences" II, 52-3.

39. *Ibid.*, 43-5.

40. Turner, n. 37, 170-80, 189; Burt, "Reminiscences" II, 53; Sulzer, n. 37, 6-7.

41. O.L. Baskin & Co., publ., *History of Clear Creek and Boulder Valleys, Colorado* (Chicago, 1880), 548; Burt, n. 38, *supra*. For Whiton, see ELB advertisement, James Sutherland et al., *Leavenworth City Directory for 1859-60* (St. Louis, 1859), 54.

42. Burt, "Reminiscences" II, 12 ff., 70, 85. Nettie's formal name was Antoinnette, but it was never used. See Edward A. Collier, *A History of Old Kinderhook* (New York & London, 1914), 474.

43. Burt, 91-2; Frederick L. Paxson, "The Railroads of the Old Northwest before the Civil War," *Transactions of the Wisconsin Academy of Science, Arts and Letters* XVII (1911), 243-67; John F. Stover, *Iron Road to the West: American Railroads in the 1850s* (New York, 1978), 136.

44. Burt, "Reminiscences" II, 91-2; letter of recommendation, N. Macneale, Aug. 10, 1854, BP.

45. Stover, *Iron Road,* 159; L.S. Nash, *Rail Road Map . . .* (Logansport, Ind., 1854), Library of Congress; Andrew M. Modelski, comp., *Railroad Maps of the United States* (Washington, 1975), 77; Burt, "Reminiscences," II, 93-4.

46. Victor M. Bogle, "Railroad Building in Indiana, 1850-1855," *Indiana Magazine of History* XLVIII, 220; Paxson, n. 45; Stover, *Iron Road,* 127 (map), 136.

47. The Rev. James H. Considine, Rector of Trinity Episcopal Church, Logansport, to the author, Dec. 5, 1978; Denver *Rocky Mountain News* (hereafter cited as *RMN*), Oct. 17, 1860; Burt, "Reminiscences" II, 12-98; Golden *Colorado Transcript* (hereafter cited as *GCT*), Aug. 21, Sept 11, 1878; *Colorado Genealogist* XI, 141, XXXVII, III, and IV, 136.

48. Burt, note 49; Helen Berthoud obituary, *GCT*, Aug. 3, 1887; Golden (Colo.) *Globe* (hereafter cited as *GG*, Aug. 6, 1887; Edward L. Berthoud obituary, *GG*, June 20, 1908.

49. Baskin, publ., *Clear Creek and Boulder Valleys,* 548; Last Will of Charles Henry Louis Berthoud, Surrogates Court, Fonda, N.Y.

ENDNOTES — CHAPTER II

1. Denver *Times*, April 11, 1908; Jay Monaghan, *Civil War on the Western Border, 1854-1865* (Boston and Toronto, 1955), 15; W. Heiss and R.T. Mayhill, eds., *The Census of the Territory of Kansas, February, 1855* (Knightstown, Ind., 1967), 23-6, 27.

2. H. Miles Moore, *Early History of Leavenworth, City and County* (Leavenworth, 1906), illustration opposite p. 180, 223.

3. Moore, 165; Leavenworth *(Weekly) Times*, April 17, 1858.

4. Report of Surveyor General of Kansas and Nebraska Territories, *Report of the Secretary of the Interior* (December 3, 1855), 308-9, 312; letter of George J. Remsburg in Leavenworth *Times*, June 18, 1908, BP; Barry, *Beginning*, 1215; Ms. Records of Kickapoo Agency, 1855, Federal Records Center, Denver.

5. ELB, *Birds*, 10; Alfred M. Bailey and Robert J. Niedrach, *Pictorial Checklist of Colorado Birds* (Denver, Colo., 1967), 77; Helena Association stock certificate, Halderman Papers KSHS; Moore, *Leavenworth*, 151-2.

6. ELB notes in Berthoud family *La Sainte Bible*, CHS; Burt, "Reminiscences" II, 98; Golden *Globe* (hereafter cited as GG), Aug. 6, 1887; the Reverend James Considine to author, Dec. 5, 1978.

7. *Reports*, Secretary of the Interior (1857), 282-3; (1858), 277, 288; (1859), 318-9; Leavenworth *Weekly Times*, Jan. 9, 1858; *Collections*, KSHS XI, 534-5 and notes.

8. *Collections*, KSHS IV, 675, XI, 534-5 and notes; N.H. Loomis, "Kansas and the Union Pacific," *Twenty-Sixth Biennial Report*, KSHS, 96-7; W.T. Sherman, *Memoirs of General W.T. Sherman* (4th edition, 2 vols., New York, 1891) I, 168-71.

9. *Collections*, KSHS XI, 534-5, XIII, 112-3; *Twenty-sixth Biennial Report*, KSHS, 96-7; George L. Anderson, *Kansas West* (San Marino, Calif., 1963), 11-15; Thomas Ewing, Jr., comp., [The Charters of the] *Leavenworth, Pawnee & Western Railroad Co.* . . . (New York, 1864, pamph.), 5-6; Leavenworth *Register*, Nov. 17, 1859, quoted in Denver *Rocky Mountain News* (hereafter cited as *RMN*), Dec. 8, 1859; ELB, *Birds*, 10; David G. Taylor, "Thomas Ewing, Jr., and the Origins of the Kansas Pacific Railway Co.," *Kansas Historical Quarterly* (hereafter cited as *KHQ*) XLII, 156-7; *Senate Executive Document* 51, Part 8, 50th Congress, 1st Session, 3852; G. Raymond Gaeddert, *The Birth of Kansas* (reprint, Philadelphia, 1974), 22, 33, 61; Allen Johnson, Dumas Malone *et al.*, eds., *Dictionary of American Biography* (hereafter cited as *DAB*) (22 vols. and supplements, New York, 1946-) VI, 238-9; *NCAB* XXV, 15.

10. Rita G. Napier, "Squatter City: The Construction of a New Community in the American West, 1854-1861" (Ph.D. dissertation, American University, 1976, in DPLW), Chapter III, esp. p. 111; James A. Rawley, *Race and Politics: Bleeding Kansas and the Coming of the Civil War* (Philadelphia and New York, 1969), 176-7; Monaghan, *Civil War*, 85; *Transactions*, KSHS IV, 522, 543, 568-9; V, 472-3; GCT, Apr. 28, 1886.

11. Burt, "Reminiscences" II, 130; Stover, *Iron Road*, 136; *RMN*, Feb. 24, 1862; Leavenworth (Weekly) *Times*, April 17, July 24, 1858; Moore, *Early History*, 172; James Sutherland *et. al.*, comps., *Leavenworth City Directory for 1859-60* (St. Louis, 1859); *Transactions*, KSHS V, 510; *Kansas Daily Ledger*, Feb. 24, 1858.

12. E.g., Leavenworth *Times*, 1858-1859, *passim*.

13. Burt, "Reminiscences" II, 130; Robert W. Baughman, comp. and ed., *Kansas in Maps* (Topeka, Kans., 1961), 42-3; George Root and Russell Hickman, "Pikes Peak Express Companies," *KHQ* XV (1946), 78 n.; *RMN*, Nov. 17, 1859; *Leavenworth City Directory* (1859-60), 54; (1860-61), 34.

14. Leavenworth *Daily Times*, Mar. 1, 2, 12, 13, 15, 17, 28, 29, 1861.

15. ELB to Thomas Ewing, Oct. 5, 1861, Leavenworth *Daily Times*, Jan. 30, 1862; *RMN*, Aug. 30, 1874.

16. Burt, "Reminiscences" II, 130; O.L. Baskin & Co., publs., *History of Clear Creek and Boulder Valleys, Colorado* (Chicago, 1880), 548; Leavenworth *Daily Times*, Mar. 24, 1860, Jan. 30, 1862, June 17, 1908; *RMN*, April 6, 11, 18, 1860, Aug. 30, 1874; Helen Berthoud obit., *GG*, Aug. 6, 1887; S.W. Burt and ELB, *The Rocky Mountain Gold Regions* (Denver City, Jefferson Territory, 1861), 21.

17. ELB, "History of Jefferson County," Baskin, publs., *History of Clear Creek and Boulder Valleys*, 365; ms. Eighth Census of the U.S., 1860, Arapaho County, Kansas Territory (Golden City), Denver Public Library hereafter citied as DPL); Golden photographs, CHS; *RMN*, Aug. 6, 20, 1859, Jan. 13, May 2, 1860; Henrietta E. Bromwell, comp., (Typescript) "Fifty-niners' Directory: Colorado Argonauts of 1858-1859" (2 vols., DPLW) I, 92; *Rocky Mountain Gold Reporter*, Sep. 10, 1859; (Golden City) *Western Mountaineer*, Dec. 7, 1859.

18. *RMN*, Oct. 17, 1860; Burt, "Reminiscences" III, 96; Burt and ELB, *Rocky Mountain Gold Regions*, 24-6; 27-8; ELB, *Birds*, 10.

19. Burt, "Reminiscences" II, 133-59; III, 2-79.

20. Ms. U.S. Census, 1860, Arapaho County, Kansas (Golden City, 585); Burt, "Reminiscences" III, 89-90, 97-98, 123, 133; Golden *Western Mountaineer*, July 19, 1860; Bliss, *Genealogy*, 256; Ward, "Colorado's only Provisional Governor," Denver *Post*, Oct. 24, 1920; Wharton, *History of Denver*, 29, 33, 65; *RMN*, May 29, 1861.

21. Burt, "Reminiscences" III, 103-4, 113, 128.

22. Burt and ELB, *Rocky Mountain Gold Regions* (see also introduction to reprinted edition by James G. Hodgson, 1962); *RMN*, Mar. 15, 1861.

23. William N. Byers, ed., *Encyclopedia of Biography and History of Colorado* (Chicago, 1901), 248-50; ms. U.S. Census, 1860, Arapaho County, Kansas (Golden City), 585; ms. U.S. Census, 1870, Jefferson County, Colo. Terr. (Golden City), 15; *Sons of Colorado* I, VI (Nov. 1906), 23; *The Colorado Magazine* (hereafter cited as CM), XXVII, 198-208; ms. First Census of the State of Colorado (Jefferson County), 1885, n.p.; ms. U.S. Census, 1880, Jefferson County, Colo. (Golden), 23.

24. ELB to Thos. Ewing, in Leavenworth *Daily Times*, Jan. 30, 1862; *KHQ* XV (1946), 78; Louise Harrison, *Empire and the Berthoud Pass* (Denver, Colo., 1964), 48 ff.; *RMN*, April 24, 1861.

25. *RMN*, May 3, 1861; Harrison, *Empire*, 55; ELB report, *RMN*, June 4, 1861; Leroy R. Hafen, *The Overland Mail, 1849-1869* (Cleveland, Ohio, 1926), 220-23 and note.

26. ELB report, *supra*; ELB to Ewing, note 8. Of the names of supplementary features, only Hoopes Creek continues on the map.

27. ELB report, note 9.

28. CM X, 189 ff.

29. *RMN*, May 29, 31, 1861.

30. Note 12; Baskin, publs., *Clear Creek and Boulder Valleys*, 368; *RMN*, June 19, 1861; J. Cecil Alter, *Jim Bridger* (new edition, 2nd printing, Norman, Okla., 1967), 297; *KHQ* XV (1946), 78-9; ELB to Thos. Ewing, Leavenworth *Daily Times*, Jan. 30, 1862.

31. *Trail* XIV, No. 5, 25; Black, *Island in the Rockies*, 39.

32. Sketch map, ELB survey book, summer 1861, BP; *RMN*, Aug. 19, 1861; ELB to Ewing, note 14.

33. ELB to Ewing, note 14; Black, *Island*, 39; ELB, *Birds*, 19-20; CM I, 139.

34. ELB (Salt Lake) to eds., *RMN*, printed in *RMN*, Aug. 19, 1861; *DAB* XVII, 386-7.

35. ELB to Ewing, note 14; *RMN*, Aug. 19, 1861. The author erred in his *Island in the Rockies* when he intimated (on p. 39) that Berthoud, as well as Vaile, made the eastbound trip by commercial stage.

36. ELB to Ewing, note 14; ELB Survey Book, summer 1861, BP.

37. *KHQ* XV (1946), 78-9; ELB Survey Book, summer 1861, BP; ELB Report, *RMN*, Oct. 12, 1861; Harrison, *Empire*, 76-9.

38. Alter, *Bridger*, 298; letter to editor, signed "Red," *RMN*, April 12, 1862.

39. CM XXVI, 85-6, IX, 164; *Trail* XII, No. 1, 11; *Official Atlas of the Civil War*, Plate CXX. Of special interest is an exquisite ms. map, completed for Bela Hughes by Redwood Fisher in 1864. The original is in the Grand County Museum, Hot Sulphur Springs, Colo.; facsimiles are in CHS and DPLW.

ENDNOTES — CHAPTER III

1. Robert Underwood Johnson and Clarence Clough Buel, eds., *Battles and Leaders of the Civil War* (4 vols., New York, 1887-1888) I, 66-71. Hereafter cited as *Battles and Leaders*.

2. *Battles and Leaders* I, 196-227.

3. *Ibid.*, 289-97, 307-13.

4. ELB obituary, GCT, June 18, 1908; Robert Lee Kerby, *The Confederate Invasion of New Mexico and Arizona, 1861-1862* (Los Angeles, 1958), Chapts. I-III.

5. Special Orders No. 2, Company H, March 23, 1862, BP.

6. Special Orders, March 23, May 14 and 19, June 17, 1862, BP; Raskin, publs., *Clear Creek and Boulder Valleys*, 371; Military Records, Frank Ferrell, Colorado State Archives (hereafter cited as CA).

7. Morris F. Taylor, "The Colorado Plains" (CHS), 7; *The War of the Rebellion: The Official Records of the Union and Confederate Armies* (128 vols., Washington, 1880-1901), Series I, Vol. XIII, 450-51 (hereafter cited as ORA).

8. ELB orders, Sept. 15, 18, 19, Oct. 8, 1862, BP.

9. ELB ms. "Journal of March of Batt 2nd Col. Inf. from Camp Weld C.T. to Ft. Lyon C.T.," BP; Hall, *Hist. of Colo.* I, 293-4; ORA Series I, Vol. XXII, Part II, 172-3.

10. Robert Lindneux, painting of Ft. Lyon, and site photos, CHS; Robert W. Frazer, *Forts of the West* (Norman, Okla., 1965), 42.

11. Ms. ELB orders, July 6, 8, Aug. 1, 1862; statements of Lt. James Burrell, GCT, Mar. 21, 28, 1877; statement of National Park Service personnel, Ft. Union National Monument, N.M., to Mrs. R.L. Chastain, October, 1978; Special Orders 111, Hqs. Dept. of N.M., June 28, 1862, File 141, CHS; *Clear Creek and Boulder Valleys*, 551.

12. ELB to Edith Shrum, September 19, 1907, BP.

13. Ms. orders, Aug. 1, Sept. 15, 18, 19, Oct. 8, 1862, BP; James Burrell in GCT, Mar. 28, 1877.

14. United States Government, *Report of the Organization of the Union Pacific R.R. Co.* (New York, 1864), 5-8.

15. Burt, "Reminiscences" IV, 74; Bromwell, comp., "Fifty-niners' Directory: Colorado Argonauts of 1858-1859" (2 vols., CHS, DPLW); Jefferson County, Colo., Book "D", 4; Book "F", 434-6, 447-8, County Clerk's office, Golden.

16. Ms. order, Dec. 13, 1862, BP; ELB orders and references, Oct., Nov., and Dec., 1862, Jan., 1863. Records of the 2nd Colorado Volunteer Cavalry (and predecessor Infantry), Military Service Records, National Archives, Washington, D.C.

17. ELB orders, Jan. 24, Feb. 20, 1863, Estate Documents, BP; ELB obit., GCT, June 18, 1908; Baskin, publs., *Clear Creek and Boulder Valleys*, 367; Grantor Book "F", Jefferson County, County Clerk's Office, Golden.

18. Ms. orders, May 2 and June 7, 1863, BP; also May 31, 1863, 2nd Colo. Cavalry Records, Military Service Records, National Archives, National Park Service, *Fort Larned National Historic Site, Kansas* (pamph.), 1976; ORA I, XXII, II, 172-3.

19. Hall, *Hist. Colo.* I, 294-5; Burrell statement, GCT, Apr. 4, 1877; ms. orders, June 18, 1863, BP; 2nd Colo. Cavalry Records (June, 1863), National Archives; DAB VI, 238-9; Hildegard Rose Herklotz, "Jayhawkers in Missouri, 1858-1863," *Missouri Historical Review* XVIII, 95-100.

20. 2nd Colo. Cav. Recs. (July-Sept., 1863), n. 19; Nat. Park Service files, Ft. Larned Nat. Monument, Kansas; (Denver) *Weekly Commonwealth*, Sept. 3, 1863; ORA I, XXII, II, 335, 347, 361, 401; ELB in GCT, Apr. 25, 1877.

21. Ms. orders, Oct. 11, Nov. 7, 26, 1863, BP; see also 2nd Colo. Cav. Records, n. 19.

22. BP; Ellen Williams, *Three Years and a Half in the Army: or, History of the Second Colorados* (New York, 1885), 37-44; Kansas City *Journal of Commerce*, Jan. 12, 1864.

23. Ms. orders, Jan. 5, 1864, BP; ELB to 2nd Lt. A. Gooding, Jan. 23, 1864, 2nd Colo. Cav. Recs., n. 19; Kansas City *Journal of Commerce*, Jan. 28, Feb. 23, 1864; *ORA* I, XXXIV, II, 364-5; ELB commission as 1st Lieutenant, BP.

24. Mark Mayo Boatner III, comp., *The Civil War Dictionary* (New York, 1959), 288; adv., *RMN*, April 23, 1859; Ford obit., *GCT*, Feb. 6, 1867; ELB statement, *GCT*, Apr. 28, 1886.

25. ELB in Baskin, *History of Arkansas Valley*, 83-4; ELB in *GCT*, Apr. 25, 1877, Apr. 28, 1886; ms. casualty figures, BP; Hall *Hist. Colo.* I, 295 ff.; Kansas City *Journal of Commerce*, Feb. 18, 19, 1864; "Permission to James M. West," West Family Papers, Jackson County Historical Society, Independence, Mo.; *ORA* I, XXXIV, II, 455-9, Part III, 93-720, *passim*, Part IV, 34, 199, 661, 710, 732.

26. Ms. orders, June 5, 13, 28, 1864, BP; ms. orders, June 2, 13, 1864, 2nd Colo. Cav. Recs., n. 19; *ORA* I, XXXIV, IV, 473.

27. U.S. Geological Survey Sheets, *Warrensburg East and Warrensburg West*, Mo., 1/24,000, 1962, also brief visits by author, 1928-1943, 1987; Prof. Roy M. Stubbs (Warrensburg) to author, Oct. 5, 1979, and post card of court house, Johnson County, Mo.; Boatner, *Civil War Dictionary*, 90; Ezra J. Warner, *Generals in Blue* (Baton Rouge, La., 1964), 48; Francis Trevelyan Miller *et al.*, eds., *Photographic History of the Civil War* (10 vols., New York, 1912) X, 217. For the Pacific R.R. see Thomas Weber, *The Northern Railroads in the Civil War, 1861-1865* (New York, 1952), 7, 39-40; *Mo. Historical Review* XVIII, 11-13; Kansas City *Journal of Commerce*, Feb. 14, Mar. 3, 1864.

28. *ORA* I, XLI, II, 409, 806-7; ms. orders, July 26, 1864, BP; ELB, in *GCT*, Apr. 25, May 2, 1877; 2nd Colo. Cavalry Recs., n. 19; Gov. John Evans (Denver) to ELB, July 22, 1864, BP; Muster-out roll, Company D, 2nd Colo. Volunteers, Book P, p. 157, CA; fragmentary ELB diary (1864), Aug. 1, 1864, BP.

29. For vivid discussions of the place of women in the western war theaters, see Williams, *Three Years and a Half in the Army*, also various issues of the regimental newspaper of the 2nd Colo., *Soldier's Letter*, esp. Volume I, No. 1; Helen Berthoud obit. in *RMN*, August 3, 1887.

30. ELB fragmentary diary (1864), Aug. 13, Sept. 1, Oct. 3, 4, 5, 6, 1864, BP; *Soldier's Letter* I, No. 5, Sept. 31 (sic!), 1864; *Mo. Hist. Rev.* VI, IV, 167-181; ms. orders, Sept. 23, Oct. 5, 1864, BP; ORA I, XLI, III, 643; (Unnamed Author), *Rebel Invasion of Missouri and Kansas* . . . (Chicago and Leavenworth, Kans., 1865), 30; Brugioni, *Civil War in Missouri*, . . . (Jefferson City, 1987), 112-18.

31. ELB in GCT, May 2, 1877; ELB diary (n. 30), Oct. 7, 8, 9, 1864; Brigioni, *Civil War in Missouri*, . . . , 118-28.

32. ORA I, XLI, I, 346, Part III, 833-92, *passim*. Part IV, 14-810, *passim:* GCT, May 2, 1877; Hall, *Hist. Colo.* IV, 369-70; ms. orders, Oct. 13, 1864, BP; ELB diary (n. 30), Oct. 14, 1864; 2nd Colo. Cavalry Records, National Archives; Weber, *Northern Railroads*, 286 n.

33. Boatner, *Dictionary*, 556; 2nd Colo. Cav. Recs. (n. 32,); *Soldier's Letter* I, No. 8, Dec. 27, 1864; Hall, *Hist. Colo.* I, 299-300.

34. ORA I, XLVIII, I, 1042; ms. orders and other papers, Jan. 31, Apr. 6, 13, 26, 29, May 14, July 24, 1865, BP. For Wise see CM VIII, 104, XIX, 137; RMN, Apr. 22, 1894; *Sons of Colorado* I, VI, 22 (Nov. 1906).

35. KHQ XLII, 329-30; *Soldier's Letter* I, No. 8, Dec. 27, 1864, No. 10, Jan. 9, 17, Feb. 24, No. 18, Mar. 4, 1865; Utley, *Frontiersmen*, 311-12.

36. Hall, *Hist. Colo.* I, 299-300; Utley, *Frontiersmen*, 311-12; ms. orders and documents, Apr. 6, 8, May 2, 3, July 9, 24, 1865, BP; Bailey and Niedrach, *Pictorial Checklist of Colorado Birds*, 77; William Frank Zornow, *Kansas: A History of the Jayhawk State* (Norman, Okla., 1957), 106-7.

37. Utley, *Frontiersmen*, 311-12; ORA I, XLVIII, II, 1038: *Soldier's Letter* I, 10, Jan. 9, 1865; 30, July 15, 1865; ELB data, 2nd Colo. Cavalry Records (n. 32,); statements, declarations, and receipts, June 20, 28, July 21, 24, Aug. 29, 1865, BP; KHQ III (1934), 253.

38. Orders and papers, June 10, 15, July 8, 9, 31, 1865, BP; ELB to George Remsburg, Jan. 27, 1905, ELB Mss., KSHS; Utley, *Frontiersmen*, 31-35; Berthoud data in 2nd Colo. Cavalry Records, June 15 and July & August, 1865 (n. 32,); O. L. Baskin, publs., *History of the City of Denver, etc.*, 2 vols. (Chicago, 1880) I, 88-9.

39. Maj. John H. Nankivel, *History of the Military Organizations of the State of Colorado, 1860-1935* (Denver, 1935), 25; *Soldier's Letter* I, 38 (Sept. 9, 30, 1865); Muster-out Roll, Company D, Book P, p. 157, CA; Berthoud data in 2nd Colo. Cavalry Records, Sept. 23, 1865 (n. 32).

40. *Soldier's Letter* I, No. 38 (Sept. 9, 1865).

41. Hall, *Hist. Colo.* IV, 370; *Real West* XVIII, No. 36, 9-64; CM XLII; Post Returns, Ft. Sedgwick (microfilm), CHS; Eugene F. Ware, "The Indian War of 1864," p. 329, CHS; photo of sketch of Ft. Sedgwick, CHS; *RMN*, Dec. 13, 27, 1865.

42. *RMN*, Mar. 13, 24, 1866; Jefferson County, Colo., Grantor Book E, 434, County Clerk's Office, Golden.

43. *RMN*, Jan. 18, Feb. 27, Mar. 8, 24, June 6, 1866; Baskin, *Clear Creek* . . . 195; Howard Fleming, *Narrow Gauge Railways in America* (2nd ed., Philadelphia, 1876, reprint by Paul Darrell, Grahame Hardy and Brian Thompson, comps. & eds., Oakland, Calif., 1949), 7-8; Hall, *Hist. Colo.* II, 407; Baskin, publs., *Denver* I, 260-63.

44. *RMN*, July 14, 23, Nov. 2, 1866; Jefferson County Grantor Book G, 209-10; CM XXVI, 86; true copy of Act of Incorporation, Colorado Central R.R., BP; Cornelius Hauck, *Narrow Gauge to Central and Silver Plume* (Golden, Colo., 1972), 16.

45. Hall, *Hist. Colo.* II, 402; Hauck, *Narrow Gauge,* 16.

46. Harrison, *Empire,* 229, 239; *RMN*, Aug. 21, 25, Sept. 1, 1866; "E.B." in *RMN*, Mar. 27, 1867.

47. *RMN*, Sept. 17, 1866; Harrison, *Empire,* 229; Hauck, *Narrow Gauge,* 16; Glenn Chesney Quiett, *They Built the West: An Epic of Rails and Cities* (New York & London, 1936), 153; Hafen, ed., *Colorado and its People* . . . (4 vols., New York, 1948) II, 638.

48. Quiett, *They Built the West,* 153; Golden *Colorado Transcript* hereafter cited as GCT), Mar. 27, 1867.

49. *RMN*, July 11, 19, Aug. 8, 9, 11, Sept. 10, 1866.

50. Hall, *Hist. Colo.* I, 384-92, II, 541-2; *RMN*, Dec. 5, 1866; R.J. Broad, "When Golden was the Capital," collected pamphlets, n.d., DPLW; GCT, Jan. 15, 1867.

51. *House Journal of the Legislative Assembly of the Territory of Colorado* (Sixth Session, Dec. 3, 1866-Jan. 11, 1867) (Central City, 1867); *RMN*, Dec. 5, 6, 13, 1866, Jan. 11, 14, 1867; Central City *Register*, Dec. 8, 1866; GCT, Dec. 19, 1866, Jan. 3, May 8, 1867.

52. *House Journal*, note 12; GCT, Jan. 16, 1867; *RMN*, May 2, 1867.

53. Treasurer's materials (1867, 1868, 1869, 1870) in BP; also GCT, Jan. 16, 1867; *RMN*, May 28, June 3, 4, 1868; obit. in GCT, June 18, 1908; *Annual Report,* Smithsonian Institution (1867), 80, 403-4, and GCT, Jan. 30, 1867. See also James D. Dana to ELB, Apr. 5, 1867, BP; GCT, May 1, 1867; Harry Adams, "Short Biography," BP; and in Joseph Ewan, *Rocky Mountain Naturalists* (Denver, 1950), 162-3.

54. Jefferson County Grantor Index Book I, 13, 15, 34; Book G, 579-80, 604-5; GCT, Jan. 30, 1867-Mar. 10, 1869, *passim*; F.W. Seward to ELB, Apr. 3, 1867, BP; Crater card indexes, DPLW; ms. U.S. Census, City of Denver, 1870, p. 43, microfilm in CHS.

55. Allen DuPont Breck, *The Episcopal Church in Colorado, 1860-1963* (Denver, 1963), 39-40; GCT, Oct. 2, 1867, June 18, 1908; ms. Calvary Church Scrapbook, Parish Office, Golden; *RMN*, Feb. 7, 1867; ms. map, "Jefferson County, C.T. 1868," CHS.

56. *Land Office Report* (1870), 425; Records in Bureau of Land Management, Denver; *Bulletin of the Nuttall Ornithological Club* II, 83; *Bulletin 44*, Agricultural College of Colorado, 160; Robert J. Niedrach and Robert B. Rockwell, *The Birds of Denver and Mountain Parks* (2nd printing, Denver, 1959); Bailey and Niedrach, *Pictorial Checklist*, 76.

57. G.L.O. Survey Books, note 17.

ENDNOTES — CHAPTER IV

1. Hafen ed., *Colo. and its People* II, 639; GCT, June 19, 1867; Minutes, C.C.R.R., pp. 1 ff., CHS; CM XVIII, 202.

2. ELB to Loveland, June 15, 1876, BP.

3. *House Journal*, Colo. Territory, Seventh Session, 35; GCT, July 3, 7, 17, 24, 1867.

4. CM XVIII, 202; Minutes of C.C.R.R. Papers, CHS, pp. 1 ff.; GCT, July 10, 1867; Hafen, ed., *Colo. and its People* II, 639-40.

5. *House Journal*, Colo. Terr., Seventh Session, 35; RMN, Aug. 22, Sept. 12, 1867; GCT, Aug. 21, Sept. 4, 11, 1867; Senate *Msc. Documents*, 40th Congress, 2nd Sess., Doc. 86, 402-3; 42nd Cong., 1st Sess., Doc. 149, 43.

6. Hafen, ed., *Colo. and its People* II, 639-40; CM XVIII, 202; ELB to Loveland, June 15, 1876, BP; GCT, Nov. 27, 1867.

7. Hauck, *Narrow Gauge*, 16; Robert M. Ormes, *Railroads and the Rockies* (Denver, 1963), 226-9; GCT, Sept. 25, Nov. 6, 27, 1867; Edward Vernon, ed., *Travelers Official Guide of the Railways*, June, 1870, table 215.

8. GCT, Nov. 27, 1867; ELB to Loveland, June 15, 1876, BP; C.C. Journal, 1870-72, Fol. 9, Box 1, C.C.R.R. Papers, pp. 4, 9, CHS; Stock Ledger, C.C.R.R. Papers. p. 14, CHS; C.C. Minutes, Fol. 3, Box 1, C.C.R.R. Papers, pp. 4-5, CHS.

9. Baskin, publs., *Clear Creek and Boulder*, 372-3; CM XXVI, 87-8, 298; Hall, *Hist. Colo.* I, 413, 437; Hauck, *Narrow Gauge*, 16, 18; *House Journal*, Colo. Terr., Seventh Session, 72-3; GCT, Jan. 8, 1868, Sept. 28, 1870; *RMN*, Sept. 22, 1870.

10. Board Minutes, C.C.R.R. Papers, CHS; Minutes of Exec. Committee, C.C.R.R., CHS; notes of C.C. Board meetings, BP; GCT, June 28, 1871, May 12, 1872; Hauck, *Narrow Gauge* 21. For Welch, see Byers, ed., *Encyclopedia.* . . . 368-70; Baskin, publs., *Clear Creek and Boulder*, 594-6, 612; ms. First Census State of Colo. (Jefferson County), 1885, Denver *Times*, Feb. 4, 1908; Dawson Scrapbooks XLVI, 85, CHS.

11. *RMN*, Apr. 4, 1870, and GCT, Apr. 6, 1870.

12. CM XXVI, 298; Hall, *Hist. Colo.* II, 420; GCT, Sept. 27, 1871; Voucher Record, Fol. 16, Box 2, C.C.R.R. Papers, CHS.

13. Fleming, *Narrow Gauge*, 14; CM XXVI, 298-304; Jefferson Construction Co. file, ELB Papers, CHS; Denver *Times*; Apr. 11, 1908; ELB Scrapbook, 24, CHS; GCT, Sept. 27, 1871; ELB, "Hist. of Jefferson County," Baskin, publs., *Clear Creek*. . ., 373; *RMN*, Aug. 15, 18, 1871.

14. GCT, June 3, 1872, Oct. 17, 1877; Tivis E. Wilkins, comp., *Colorado Railroads: Chronological Development* (Boulder, Colo. 1974), 25; Baskin publs., *Clear Creek*. . ., 374.

15. Exec. Committee Minutes, C.C.R.R. Papers, Box 1, Fol. 4, CHS; ELB Scrapbook, pp. 32, 36, 38, CHS; *RMN*, Oct. 14, 1871; Davis, *First Five Years*, 162-3.

16. Baskin, *Clear Creek*, 373. Right of Way File C 0122071 (Colo. Central R.R.), BLM, Denver.

17. Baskin, *Clear Creek*. . ., 373; C.C. Welch to T.E. Sickles, Nov. 25, 1872, Colo. Improvement Co. Letter Book, Box 2, Fol. 20, C.C.R.R. Papers, CHS; GG, Apr. 5, 26, 1873; GCT, Apr. 23, 1873; E.W. Rollins to E.H. Rollins, Oct. 23, 1874, Colo. Imp. Co. Letter Book (Mar. 1874 to Jan. 1876 and Jan. 1882), Box 2, Fol. 21, C.C.R.R. Papers, CHS; rough notes, July 1873, BP.

18. Denver & South Platte files, BP; Baskin, *Clear Creek*, 373, 596; Jefferson Construction Co. file, BP; ELB Scrapbook, 74, 86, CHS; Minutes of C.C. Board, Box 1, Fols. 41-2, C.C.R.R. Papers, CHS; Minutes of C.C. Exec. Committee, C.C.R.R. Papers, Box 1, Fol. 4, CHS.

19. See citations in note 17, *supra;* also *Map of the Colo. Central Railroad 1878,* BP; *RMN,* Mar. 12, 1873; ELB, *Colo. Central R.R. "Itinerary," 1873 and 1874* . . . (St. Louis, 1873), 3; GG, Apr. 19, Aug. 2, 1873; Grantor Index 2, Sec. B, County Clerk, Jefferson County.

20. Byers, ed., *Encyclopedia* . . . , 369; Jefferson Construction Co. file, BP; Letter Book, Colorado Improvement Co., Fol. 21, Box 2, C.C.R.R. Papers, CHS.

21. Jefferson Construction Co. file, BP; also "Sub Voucher" file, BP.

22. ELB, *Colorado Central Itinerary, passim.*

23. Stock Ledger, C.C.R.R., p. 14, CHS; C.C.R.R. Ledger Balances, 1876-86, Fol. 14, Box 1, C.C.R.R. Papers, CHS; CM XXVI, 304; GG, May 3, 1873; *100 Years* (Golden souvenir pamphlet, Golden, Colo., 1959), 11; Baskin, *Clear Creek* . . . , 373; Jefferson Construction Co. file, BP.

24. E.W. Rollins to Mike Hawlett, July 22, 1875, Letter Book (Mar. 1874-July 1876) of Colo. Improvement Co., p. 156, Fol. 21, Box 2, C.C.R.R. Papers, CHS; Jeff. Constr. Co. file, BP; GCT, Oct. 21, 1874. But see Wilkins, *Colorado Railroads* for 1.7 miles of track laying in 1879.

25. Golden & South Platte file, BP; Wilkins, *Colo. Railroads,* 11, 13, 16-17; GCT, May 8, 1872; Wilkins, *Colo. Railroads,* 27, 111.

26. The ultimate power of eastern finance becomes repeatedly evident in BP and the C.C.R.R. records in CHS.

27. J.R. Perkins, *Trails, Rails and War,* 262-3; also typed reminiscences of E.L. Jones, Fol. 18, Box 2, C.C.R.R. papers, CHS.

28. Ormes, *Railroads and the Rockies,* 277; Hall, *Hist. Colo.* II, 407-8, 420; Baskin, *Clear Creek* . . . , 197.

29. GCT, Aug. 23, 1876; GG, Aug. 19, 1876; Sen. *Exec. Docs.* 51, Part 5, 50th Congress, 1st Sess., 1848-9.

30. Hall, *Hist. Colo.* II, 408-9, 411; minutes of ELB, May 18, 1876, BP, also copies in C.C.R.R. Papers, Fol. 4, Box 1, CHS.

31. Hall, *Hist. Colo.* II, 408-11; C.C. Board Minutes, May 18, 1876, C.C.R.R. Papers, CHS; Baskin, *Clear Creek* . . . , 373-4; ELB notes and minutes, May 18, 1876, BP; GCT, May 24, 1876; GG, May 20, 1876.

32. See, generally, citations in note 31, *supra.*

33. Hall, *Hist. Colo.* II 411; GCT, May 24, 1876.

34. Hall, *Hist. Colo.* II, 411-12; GCT, May 24, 1876, GG, May 27, 1876.

35. Hall, *Hist. Colo.* II, 413, 419 ff.; GCT, June 17, 28, 1876.

36. Ms. ELB C.C. minutes, Aug. 14, 1876, BP; Hall, *Hist. Colo.* II, 413-19; CM XVII, 19-26; *Saga* I, V, 46 ff. (Jan., 1951); GCT, Aug. 16, 23, 1876; GG, Aug. 19, 1876.

37. Hall, *Hist. Colo.* II, 415-19; C.C. Minutes, Aug. 14, 1876, BP; GCT, Aug. 16, 23, 1876; Baskin, publs., *Clear Creek . . .* , 374; ms. C.C. financial sheet, 1876, BP; ELB to Porter, Bell & Co., Oct. 18, 1876, BP.

38. Berthoud postal correspondence, Aug. 21, 1876-July 25, 1877, ms. letter press, BP; GCT, Aug. 9, 16, 1876.

39. Baskin, *Clear Creek . . .* 197; Hall, *Hist. Colo.* II, 413; GG, Aug. 19, 1876.

40. Sen. *Exec. Doc.* 51, Part 4, 50th Congress, 1st Sess., p. 1741; Hall, *Hist. Colo.* II, 422.

41. Hall, *op. cit.*, 422; ELB to Thos. J. Brady, July 25, 1877, BP.

42. *RMN*, Mar. 11, 13, 1877.

43. *RMN*, Mar. 13, 1877; E.L. Jones, "Extending the old Colorado Central Lines" (typed reminiscences), Fol. 18, Box 2, C.C.R.R. Papers, CHS; ELB, *Birds*, 10; Alfred M. Bailey and Robert J. Niedrach, *Birds of Colorado* (2 vols., Denver, 1965) I, 403.

44. Right of Way File C0122173, BLM, Denver; CM XXVI, 88; Belva Turner Bashor *et al.*, *Early Berthoud; a History of a Town* (Ft. Collins, Colo., 1976), 1-2; Hall, *Hist. Colo.* IV, 189.

45. Jones, note 43, *supra*; Hall, *Hist. Colo.* II, 422-23; Baskin, *Clear Creek . . .* , 374; C.C. Directors' Minutes, Apr. 9, 1877, BP; GG, July 8, 1876, Mar. 17, 31, Apr. 7, May 19, 1877.

46. Julius Grodinsky, *Jay Gould: His Business Career, 1867-1892* (New York, 1916), 142-3, 179; Jones, note 43, *supra*; Hall, *Hist. Colo.* II, 423-4; Senate *Exec. Doc.* 51, Part 4, 50th Congress, 1st Sess., p. 1740. ELB letter press, note and minutes, 1877-1879, BP; C.C.R.R. papers, Box 1, Fols. 4-6 and Letter Book, 1st Mortgage Bonds, CHS; GCT, Jan. 1, Apr. 15, 16, 1879; GG, June 26, 1878.

47. C.C.R.R. Papers, Box 1, Fols. 4-6; Box 2, Fols. 22-25, CHS; ELB letter press notes and minutes, C.C.R.R., BP; GG, May 31, June 28, Aug. 2, 1879.

ENDNOTES — CHAPTER V

1. Ms. Report, "Black Hills" Survey, May 28, 1878, BP; GG, May 15, 1878.

2. Ibid,; also "Notes of Black Hills Survey", BP; *The Botanical Gazette* XI (Oct., 1892), 3, 21; Lilian L. Fitzpatrick, *Nebraska Place Names* (Lincoln, 1964), 89, 181-2; Rand McNally & Co., *Pioneer Atlas of the American West* (Chicago, New York, and San Francisco, 1956), 13.

3. Ms. Report, "Black Hills" Survey; GCT, June 19, 1878; *Senate Exec. Doc. 51, Part 9, 59th Cong., 1st Session,* 5287.

4. Merrill D. Beal, *Intermountain Railroads: Standard and Narrow Gauge* (Caldwell, Idaho, 1962), 20, 27, 37, 41, 56, 59, 76-7, 79-80; *Sen. Exec. Docs., 51, Part 2, 50th Cong., 1st Sess.,* 537, 571; Athearn, *Union Pacific Country,* 253-5; Rand McNally & Co., *Pioneer Atlas . . .,* 10; General Land Office, *Map of Terr. of Idaho* (1883); *Idaho Yesterdays* XIX, I, 2; Hubert Howe Bancroft, *Works* XXI (*Washington, Idaho, and Montana*) (San Francisco, 1890), 684 ff.; Clark C. Spence, ed., *Territorial Politics and Government in Montana* (Urbana, Chicago, and London, 1975), 116 ff.

5. Helena *Daily Independent,* June 26, 1878; GCT, June 12, 19, 26, July 3, 31, 1878; GG, Oct. 2, 1878.

6. *Colorado Rail Annual No. 15* (Golden, Colo., 1981), 33 (photo); Rand McNally, *Pioneer Atlas . . .,* 10; Gen. Land Office map, *Terr. of Idaho* (1879); U.S. Geological Survey, *Arimo, Ida.,* sheet (1968); GCT, June 26, 1878; Helena *Daily Herald,* July 1, 1878, and following issues.

7. Pay Roll, Utah & Northern Railroad Extension, June 1878, BP; Vouchers File No. 2, U. & N. R.R., BP; telegram, ELB to Gould, Aug. 13, 1878, BP; Bill, James Packer, Aug. 12, 1878, BP; Expense Account, ELB to "Mr. Clark" (U.P. Gen. Supt.), Oct. 24, 1878, BP; Level Book No. 1, E.L. Jones, BP; Salt Lake News, Jan. 18, 1919; Dawson Scrapbooks XLVI, 42, CHS; GCT, June 26, Oct. 30, 1878.

8. Report, ELB to Jay Gould, Aug. ?, 1878, also Level Books Nos. 1 and 2, E.L. Jones, BP; U.S. Geological Survey, Monida, Montana-Idaho sheet (1968); Kansas City Review V, No. 10, 588; GCT, Sept. 25, Oct. 30, 1878; Helena Daily Independent, July 3, Aug. 6, 1878; Salt Lake News, Jan. 18, 1919; Colo. Rail Annual No. 15 (1981), 15, 38, also 57, 92, and 129 (photos).

9. Level Book No. 2, note 8; Salt Lake News, Jan. 18, 1919; ELB to Gould, n. 8; Transit Book No. 6, Stinking Water Route (1878), BP.

10. Beal, Intermountain Railroads, 83; Strip Map Books (U. & N.), BP; ms. ELB eclipse notes, July 29, 1878, BP.

11. U.S. Geological Survey, Dalys, Mont., sheet (1952); ELB eclipse notes, July 29, 1878, BP; GCT, July 31, 1878; Missoula Weekly Missoulian, Aug. 2, 1878; Helena Daily Independent, July 30, Aug. 9, 1878.

12. Citations in n. 11.

13. Report, ELB to Gould, Aug. ?, 1878, BP; Salt Lake News, Jan. 18, 1919; Helena Daily Herald, July 1-Aug. 6, 1878; ELB to Gould, Aug. 13, 1878, BP.

14. ELB to Gould, Aug. 13, 1878, supra; Joseph Luce to ELB (Aug. 29, 1878), BP; U. & N. Voucher No. 2, (Aug. 12, 1878), BP; telegrams, Milner to ELB, Aug. 19, 29, 1878, BP; draft of report, ELB to Gould, n. 13, U. & N. Transit Book No. 2 and Level Notes No. 4, BP; Helena Daily Herald, Aug. 12, 19, 1878; Helena Daily Independent, Aug. 17, 1878; Spence, Territorial Politics, 116 ff.

15. Beal, Intermountain Railroads, 76-7, 80 and n.; Montana History XVIII (4), 6 and illus., 9-16; ELB bill to U. & N. Survey Account, Sept. 1, 1878, BP; telegram, Gould to ELB, Aug. 22, 1878, BP; Spence, Territorial Politics, 116-129; Gould to Hauser, Aug. 22, 1878, Hauser Papers, Box 4, File 44, Montana State Historical Society; Weekly Missoulian, Sept. 6, 1878; Helena Daily Independent, June 28, 1878; Helena Daily Herald, July 24, Sept. 2, 21, 1878.

16. ELB bill, n. 15; *GCT*, Sept. 11, 25, 1878; Helena *Daily Herald*, Aug. 23, Sept. 5, 1878; various survey notebooks, BP; *Montana History* (note 15), 20.

17. ELB expense account, Sept. 22, 1878, BP; exchange draft, Sept. 30, 1878, BP; *GCT*, Sept. 25, Oct. 30, 1878; Madison *Madisonian*, Oct. 5, 1878; Helena *Daily Independent*, Sept. 14, 1878; Weekly *Missoulian*, Aug. 23, Sept. 13, 1878.

18. Expense account, R.R. Williams, Oct. 24, 1878, BP; receipted bills for rifles and cartridges, Sept. 14, 1878, BP; draft of letter, ELB to Gould, Aug. ?, 1878, BP; U.&N. Transit Notes Book No. 3, BP; Level Notes, Homeward Bound No. 2, BP; *Weekly Missoulian*, Sept. 13, 1878; *K.C. Review* V, No. 10, 587; Salt Lake *News*, Jan. 18, 1919; Helena *Daily Independent*, Sept. 14, 1878.

19. *Record of Proceedings*, Davenport Academy of Natural Sciences, 83-8; U. & N. Transit Notes Book No. 3, BP; *Kansas City Review* V, No. 10, 587-9; F. V. Hayden, *Reports* XII, Part II, 63; Salt Lake *News*, Jan. 18, 1919.

20. ELB Expense Account, Oct. 23, 1878, and U. & N. Transit Notes Book No. 3, BP; *Proceedings*, Davenport Academy, n. 19; *K.C. Review* V, No. 10. 5879; *GCT*, Oct. 23, 1878; Salt Lake *News*, Jan. 18, 1919.

21. *GCT*, Sept. 18, Nov. 13, 1878. See also Payroll, U. & N. Extension, Nov., 1878; cancelled checks, U. & N. Engineering Acct., Nov., 1878; ELB to S.H.H. Clark, Nov. 27, 1878; ELB to Gould, with reports, Nov. 30, 1878; all of these in BP.

22. Helena *Daily Independent*, Sept. 14, Oct., 3, 4, 5, 1878, Jan. 15-Mar. 26, 1879; Hubert Howe Bancroft, *History of Montana, Idaho and Washington* (San Francisco, 1890), 684-7; Beale, *Intermountain Railroads*, 92-3, 124; Abdill, *Pacific Slope Railroads*, 95-6.

23. GG, Oct. 2, 1878; receipted bills of Milner party, fall of 1878, BP; printed articles of incorporation, G.L. & S.J., BP; copy of report of G.L. & S.J. officers, Sept. 1, 1879, *ibid.*; *GCT*, Nov. 20, Dec. 4, 18, 1878, Jan. 1, 14, 1879.

24. Hall, *Hist. Colo.* II, 424; ELB to Gould, Feb. 12, 1879 and C.C. Directors' Minutes, Feb. 17, Mar. 18, 29, 1879, BP; GG, Feb. 22, Mar. 8, 1879.

25. GCT, Mar. 26, Apr. 2, 16, 30, May 28, June 4, July 2, 23, Aug. 20, 1879; Pay Records, Mar., 1879, BP; Labor Check Roll C.C.R.R., and U.P. Time Roll, June, 1879, BP; List of articles and other expenses, June, July, 1879, expense account and U.P. time roll, "G. & L. R.R.," Aug., 1879, ibid,; draft letter ELB to Auditor of C.C. and U.P., Aug. 31, 1879, ibid.; Transit Note Books and Strip Map Books, ibid.; U.S. Geological Survey, Mt. Harvard, Colo., sheet, 1955.

26. GCT, Apr. 30, May 14, 28, July 2, 9, 12, 23, Aug. 20., Oct. 1, 1879; GG, June 28, 1879; Leadville Chronicle, July 18, 1879; Georgetown Courier, July 31, 1879; ELB to F.W. Gannett, Aug. 31, Oct. 16, 1879, BP.

27. GG, Oct. 2, 1878, Aug. 2, Sept. 6, 1879; hotel receipt, Dec. 10, 1878, BP; GCT, July 9, 16, 23, Aug. 20, 1879; CM XXIV, V, 1881-90; ms. Map of G.B. & L. Ry., Georgetown to Loveland Pass, R/W R.R. Case, File C-0122163, BLM, Denver; 134 I.C.C. Reports, 616, 687.

28. Ms. estimates (High Line), BP; 134 I.C.C. Reports, 616, 6878; GCT, Apr. 30, 1879, June 18, 1908; "Preliminary Berthoud" profile, Loveland Pass to Evans Gulch, undated, Colorado & Southern engineering records, Xerox copy in Colo. Railroad Museum, Golden; ms. "Plan A" section, Loveland Pass Tunnel, May 10, 1882, BP; also Georgetown Courier, July 31, 1879; Georgetown Miner, Aug. 2, 1879; RMN, July 27, 1879; Senate Exec. Doc. 51, Part 9, 50th Congress, 1st Session, 5286; ms. Map of G.B. & L. Ry., Georgetown to Loveland Pass, R/W R.R. Case, File C-0122163, BLM, Denver; 134 I.C.C. Reports, 688; CM XXIV, V, 1881-90.

29. Salary statements, Dec. 28, 1880, Feb. 28, 1881, BP; GCT, Oct. 1, 1879; RMN, Jan. 25, July 20, 23, 1881; GG, Mar. 5, 1881; CM XXIV, V, 188; Henry McFarland to ELB, Dec. 8 and 9, 1882, Transfer Documents to A.A. Egbert, Dec. 20, 1882, resignation of ELB to Sidney Dillon, Dec. 4, 1882, reply of Dillon to ELB, Dec. 11, 1882, all in BP. See also transfer of shares, ELB to F.L. Ames, Dec. 11, 1882, Stock Ledger, C.C.R.R. Papers, CHS, p. 14.

30. GG, April 5, 1879; Ormes, Railroads and the Rockies, 153, 261; GCT, May 7, 21, 1879, Aug. 25, 1880; RMN, Aug. 26, 1880; "G.G. and Central R.R." Book, 1876-1883, BP.

31. Level Book, Reconnaissance to Estes Park, April, 1880, BP; Henry Adams, The Education of Henry Adams (Modern Library Edition, New York, 1931), 311; RMN, July 23, 1881, July 18, 1883; Ormes, Railroads, 163; Del Norte Transit and Level Books, Oct.-Nov., 1882, BP. RMN, Mar. 17, 18, May 11, June 11, Oct. 4, 14, 1881; also Ormes, Railroads, 208, and sketch map and grade profile, upper Cache la Poudre, BP.

32. *American Journal of Science* (Feb., 1876), 108-111; *Record of Proceedings, Davenport Academy of Natural Sciences*, 81-8; *Kansas City Review of Science and Industry* V, I, (May, 1881). Elbert Little, Jr., *Check List of Native and Naturalized Trees of the United States* (Washington, Govt. Printing Office, 1953), 27-30, 37, 98, 219, 255, 258, 281, 284, 378, 391.

33. *Kansas City Reviews of Science* (hereafter cited as *KCRS*) VII (1883), No. 8, 489-90; *Fourth Annual Report*, Bureau of Ethnology (1886), 27-8.

34. *KCRS* III, IV, 536-8, 652-4: VI, 218-19, 536-40; Baskin, *Clear Creek and Boulder Valleys*, 365; *GCT*, Dec. 3, 1879; *RMN*, Oct. 8, 1881.

35. *RMN*, June 24, 1868; obit. of Old, Denver *Republican*, Apr. 18, 1901; Hayden *Reports* VI, 97, 106n., 126, 136; VII, 365, 368-9; X, 311, 320, 339; U.S. Geological Survey, *Minerals, Lands and Geology* . . . I (Before 1879), 256; Henry Adams, *Education* . . . , 310 ff.

36. Baskin, *Clear Creek and Boulder*, portrait facing p. 72; Lt. Col. John Whittemore to Jas. L. Norris, Jan 28, 1884 and pertinent papers, BP; Lupo, *Waymarks*, 148; Lupo to author, Feb. 15, 1979; Dec., 1883, weather chart, BP; ELB, *Statistical Review of Jefferson County, Colo.* (1882); ms. Calvary Parish Register, 96-9; *RMN*, Mar. 10, 1881, Feb. 12, 1882.

37. *GCT*, May 6, 1874, May 5, Oct. 6, 1875; GG, June 24, 1896; *Colo. Business Directory* (1875), 171, (1876), 177, (1877), 167, (1878), 147; ELB obit., *GCT*, June 18, 1908.

38. Jessee R. Morgan, *World School: The Colorado School of Mines* (Denver, 1955), 64-5, 184; Breck, *Episcopal Church in Colorado*, 57; Neil W. Kimball, "George West," CM XXVII, 204.

39. *Ibid.*

40. *Ibid.* See also *RMN*, Oct. 19, 1870, Aug. 27, 1872; Ewan, *Rocky Mtn. Naturalists*, 53-4; Morgan, *World School*, 74-77; *GCT*, Oct. 28, Dec. 3, 1874, Feb. 17, 1875.

41. Blake, publ. *Colo. Business Directory* (1875), 34; Moran, *World School*, 65-6, 78, 80-85; GG, Jan. 29, 1876, June 6, 1883; *GCT*, Sept. 15, 1875, Apr. 2, 1879; Baskin, *Clear Creek and Boulder*, 377; *Catalog*, CSM (1882), 57.

42. Wallihan, *Directory* (1871), 324; ELB Scrapbook, file 86, also signed receipt, Oct. 12, 1876, BP; and Denver *Times*, April 11, 1908; Notebooks and Ditch Level Book, "G.D. and Flume Co., 1886, No. 2," BP; GG, April 21, 1883; 134 I.C.C. *Reports*, 689-90; Wilkins, *Colorado Railroads*, 55.

43. *Colo. Business Directory* (1875) 23, (1876) 43, (1877) 22, (1878) 24; "Ditch Levels" Book, 1886, BP; GG, May 13, 1876; GCT, Jan. 13, Aug. 18, Sept. 22, 1875; *RMN*, Sept. 14, 1880; mining claim, Shamrock Lode, BP; Jefferson County Grantor and Grantee Books and Indexes, 1868-1887, *passim*; ms. U.S. Census data, Jefferson County (Golden City), 15-351; GCT, May 13, Jan. 6, Oct. 21, 1874; "Legal Titles . . . Jefferson County," typescript, DPL, WHD (Jefferson County, 6); CM XIV, 175.

44. Ms. Tenth Census of the U.S., Jefferson County, Colo. (Golden), p. 32; ms. Colo. State Census, 1885, Jefferson County, District ; 1, p. 30; Jackson Printing Co., *Colo. State Business Directory* (1881), 238; Crocker, H.S. & Co., *McKenney's Business Directory of the Principal Towns of Utah, Colo. (et al.)* (1882), 956; James R. Ives, *Colo. State Business Directory* (1888), 331; Baskin, *Denver* II, 83-9; GCT, Sept. 1, 1880, Feb. 14, 1887; Baskin, *Clear Creek and Boulder Valleys*, 377; *RMN*, May 31, 1882, July 17, 18, 1883, Aug. 1, 1886; Kay R. Merrill, ed., *Colo. Collections*, IV, Foothills Genealogical Society; ms. Calvary Parish Register, 14, 21.

45. *"La Sainte Bible,"* BP; *RMN*, Aug. 3, 1887; Denver *Times*, Aug. 2, 1887; Denver *Republican*, Aug. 3, 1887; GCT, Aug. 3, 1887; GG, Aug. 6, 1887.

ENDNOTES — CHAPTER VI

1. ELB, *Birds*, 11; GCT, Jan. 29, 1890, June 18, 1908; Ms. Calvary Parish Register, 33; GG, Apr. 11, June 20, 1908; Denver *Times*, Apr. 11, 1908.

2. *The Purple and Gold* (Chi Psi Magazine) LV, No. 2 (Jan. 1938), 92; Denver *Times*, April 11, 1908; GCT, June 18, 1908.

3. Charles S. Ryland, ". . . Berthoud," *Denver Westerners Monthly Roundup*, XXI, Nos. 9 and 10, p. 9; GCT, June 4, 16, Dec. 24, 1890.

4. ELB, *A Sketch of the Natchez Indians* (Golden, Colo., 1886, pamphlet); ELB, *Birds, Their Geological History, Migrations and Uses* (Golden, Colo., 1887, pamphlet); *Bulletin 44*, State Agricultural College (March, 1889); Bailey and Niedrach, *Birds of Colorado*.

5. "E.B." in CM, I, 139; ELB, *The Botanical Gazette*, XI (Oct. 1892), 321-6; ELB, *The Ice Age and Pliocene Man* (Pamphlet, n.d. — c. 1905).

6. Hall, *Hist. Colo.*, II, 246; ms. "Notice," April 1888, BP; *National Geographic Magazine*, VI, 209-14 (Dec. 29, 1894).

7. ELB, *The Boundaries of Louisiana in 1803* (Golden, Colo., 1897, pamphlet); *Gulf Magazine*, I (1902), 128-33; Richardson and Morse, comps., *Writings on American History, 1902* (Princeton, N.J., 1904), 122.

8. ELB, "The Sea of the West and Vérendrye's Journal" (with penciled notation, not in ELB's hand, indicating typewritten and carbon copies were made), BP.

9. File 15, "Correspondence, 1903," BP; *Transactions,* KSHS, VIII, 438 n.; Edw. A. Kilian to ELB, Aug. 15, 1902, attached to Vérendrye ms., BP; ms. copy, "Danebert's Map, 1661," BP; ELB to George J. Remsburg, Jan. 27, 1905, ELB Mss., KSHS; George J. Remsberg to Leavenworth *Times,* June 18, 1908, photocopy in BP.

10. GG, Apr. 4, 1891.

11. GG, Apr. 4, 5, 11, May 31, June 7, Aug. 16, 1890, Jan. 10, Mar. 21, 28, 1891; GCT, Apr. 2, 8, May 21, 28, 1890, Mar. 25, Apr. 1, 1891.

12. Breck, *Episcopal Church,* 83; GCT, Jan. 29, 1890, special resumé edition, Oct. 1898, Nov. 22, 1899, June 13, 1900; ms. Calvary Parish Register, 6-9, 104-5, 200-07.

13. GG, Feb. 25, 1899; *Catalog,* CSM, 1882, 1885-6, 1887-8, *et seq.*; Morgan, *World School,* 137; "County Road Nov. 1888" Notebook, BP; Golden Weather Records, Feb. 16 through June, 1895, BP.

14. *Catalog,* CSM, 1899-1900, 5-7, 17, 73; 1901-02, 5-7, 8, 73; GG, Feb. 24, 900, April 18, 25, 1903.

15. GCT, May 28, 1903.

16. *Catalog,* CSM, 1902-03, 6-7; GG, Apr. 18, 25, May 8, 1903; GCT, May 28, 1903.

17. Oral information supplied by CSM Alumni Office, December 5, 1978; CSM *Quarterly,* XII, No. 1 (*Catalog Edition*), 1917, p. 131; Morgan, *World School,* 138; GCT, May 27, 1903; GG, May 30, 1903, May 27, 1905.

18. G. & D. RR Levels, Preliminary Book 1; D.L. and Golden RR 1890 survey book; Preliminary Survey and Level Notebooks (1890); also County Road Notebook, Nov. 1888, BP; GG, Sept. 27, 1890, Jan. 3, Sept. 5, 26, 1891; GCT, Oct. 1, 1890, Feb. 4, 1891; R.A. LeMassena, *Colorado's Mountain Railroads,* V (Golden, 1966), 164-5, 175; Wilkins, *Colorado Railroads,* 88, 103, 114.

19. Notebook, "County Rd. Nov. 1888," with addenda, also "Golden and Denver" notebook (first dated Nov. 3, 1887), BP; GCT, Dec. 18, 1889; GG, Mar. 29, 1890; "Level Book S. Boulder & Ralston Creek," July 14-22, 1898, BP; U.S. Geol. Survey Special Map, *Denver Mountain Area* (1950); untitled level book, beginning Aug. 29, 1899, BP.

20. GCT, June 18, 1903, Jan. 21, Apr. 21, 1904, Apr. 3, 1908; E.O. Hovey, to ELB, May 4, 1907, BP; Rosalie Burnap to A.D. Jameson, Nov. 2, 1908, ELB Estate Papers, CSA; GCT, June 18, 1908; George M. Kimball *et al.,* *Illustrated Golden and Vicinity* (Golden, Colo., 1902); RMN, Mar. 1, 1908.

21. GG, April 11, 1908; Denver *Times*, Apr. 11, 1908; check stubs, ELB Estate Account, CSA.

22. Denver *Times*, Apr. 11, 1908.

23. A.D. Jameson to Elsie B. Hoyle, July 14, 1908, ELB Estate Papers, CSA; *Trail*, I, No. 1, 25; GCT, June 11, 18, 1908.

24. Ms. Calvary Parish Register, 216-7.

25. GCT, June 18, 1908; Denver *Republican*, June 14, 15, 1908; RMN, June 14, 1908; Denver *Times*, June 15, 1908.

26. GCT, June 18, 1908; GG, June 20, 1908; Denver *Republican*, June 14, 1908; ms. Calvary Parish Register, 216-7.

27. Ms. Calvary Parish Register, 216-7; A. D. Jameson (Administrator) to Elsie B. Hoyle Tidball, July 14, 1908, ELB Estate Papers, CSA; Administrator's reports, *ibid.*; Jameson to W.E. Greenlee, May 17, 1909, *ibid.*; ms. explanation, attached to Salt Lake City-Denver Field notes, Aug. 9-Sept. 17, 1861, BP; Rosalie Burnap to A.D. Jameson, Nov. 2, 1908, ELB Estate Papers, CSA.

28. Grace Jameson Rowe to Colo. Editor, RMN, Nov. 24, 1953, copy with four-page essay, Golden Historical Museum.

BIBLIOGRAPHY

MANUSCRIPT AND ARCHIVAL MATERIAL

Edward L. Berthoud Collection.
Colorado School of Mines Library, Golden, Colorado.
Edward L. Berthoud Collection.
Kansas State Historical Society, Topeka.
Edward L. Berthoud Papers.
Colorado Historical Society, Denver.
Bureau of Indian Affairs, Kickapoo Agency Records.
Federal Archives and Records Center, Denver, Colorado.
Bureau of Land Management Records.
Denver, Colorado.
Silas Wright Burt Collection.
New York Historical Society, New York.
Calvary Church Records.
Golden, Colorado.
Census Records: Seventh, Eighth, Ninth, and Twelth Censuses.
Copies and Microfilm in Colorado Historical Society, Denver;
Denver Public Library; and New York Historical Society, New York.
E.H. Collins Collection.
Colorado Historical Society, Denver.
Colorado Central Railroad Papers.
Colorado Historical Society, Denver.
Colorado State Archives, Denver.
Colorado & Southern Engineering Records.
Colorado Railroad Museum, Golden.

Geological Survey Records.
National Archives, Washington, D.C.
Georgetown, Breckenridge & Leadville Railroad Papers.
Colorado Historical Society, Denver.
Golden City Association Records.
Colorado Historical Society, Denver.
Grand County Museum Archives.
Hot Sulphur Springs, Colorado.
Samuel F. Hauser Collection.
Montana State Historical Society, Helena.
Index, The Reformed Church, Fort Plain, New York.
Department of History and Archives, Montgomery County, Fonda, New York.
Jefferson County Clerk Records.
Golden, Colorado.
Lutheran Trinity Church Records.
Department of History and Archives, Montgomery County, Fonda, New York.
Military Service Records.
National Archives, Washington, D.C.
National Park Service Files.
Fort Larned National Monument, Kansas.
Panama Railroad Company, TPV/v Manuscript Collection.
New York Public Library.
Post Reports and Returns, Fort Sedgwick, Colorado.
Colorado Historical Society, Denver.
Records of Second Colorado Volunteer Cavalry (and predecessor Infantry).
Military Service Records, National Archives, Washington, D.C.
Records of Vital Statistics, Palatine, New York.
Department of History and Archives, Fonda, New York.
Surrogate's Court.
Montgomery County, Fonda, New York.
James West Family Papers.
Jackson County Historical Society, Independence, Missouri.

MAPS AND ATLASES (PUBLISHED)

Baskin, Forster & Company, compilers.
Illustrated Historical Atlas of the State of Indiana. Chicago, 1876.

Baughman, Robert W., compiler and editor.
Kansas in Maps. Topeka, Kansas, 1961.

DeWitt, Simeon, publisher.
Map of the City and County of New York (1832). (Map Division, NYPL).

General Land Office.
Map of the Territory of Idaho (1879).

Hamilton, John, printer.
Map of the Colorado Central Rail Road 1878. New York, 1878.

Harrison, Thomas. (Crown Surveyor, Jamaica), delineator.
Isthmus of Panama, 1855. Map and Profile of the Panama R.R. and Adjoining Country from Limon or Navy Bay on the Atlantic Ocean to the Bay of Panama on the Pacific Ocean. (Printed facsimile in Map Division, NYPL).

Nash, L.S., Chief Engineer.
Rail Road Map Accompanying the Report and Exhibit of the Chief Engineer of the Logansport and Northern Indiana Railroad . . . (Logansport, Indiana, May 1, 1854; copy in Library of Congress).

Rand McNally & Company, compiler.
Pioneer Atlas of the American West. Chicago, 1956.

Socolofsky, Homer E., and Hubee Self, compilers.
Historical Atlas of Kansas. Norman, Oklahoma, 1972.

U.S. Geological Survey.
(Special Map) *Denver Mountain Area* (1950).

U.S. Geological Survey.
Quadrangle Sheets, various areas, dates, and scales.

Untitled.
"Cholera Centers in New York City (1832)." (Map Division, NYPL).

Yoseloff, reprinter.
The Official Atlas of the Civil War. New York, 1958.

PUBLIC DOCUMENTS (FEDERAL) UNITED STATES

Hayden, Ferdinand V., compiler.
Preliminary Field Report of the United States Geological Survey of Colorado and New Mexico (1869). (Washington, 1869.) (First volumes of a set of 12).

Hayden, Ferdinand V., compiler.
Reports of the United States Geological and Geographical Survey of the Territories.
(12 vols., 1871-1883).

Interstate Commerce Commission.
Reports.

Land Office Report. (Washington, 1870.)

Little, Elbert L., Jr.
Check List of Native and Naturalized Trees of the United States. (Washington, 1953.)

Report of the U.S. Pacific Railway Commission, Senate Ex. Doc. 51, 50th Congress, 1st Session.

Rabbit, Mary C., for United States Geological Survey.
Minerals, Lands and Geology for the Common Defense and General Welfare (Volume 1, Before 1879) (Washington, 1979).

Annual Report of the Board of Regents of the Smithsonian Institution. (Washington, D.C., 1867, 1876).

U.S. Senate.
Executive Documents.

United States.
Executive Documents. Reports of the Secretary of the Interior.

United States of America.
Report of the Organization and Proceedings of the Union Pacific Railroad Company. (New York, 1864).

The War of the Rebellion: The Official Records of the Union and Confederate Armies. (128 vols., Washington, Government Printing Office, 1880-1901.) (Cited herein as ORA).

PUBLIC DOCUMENTS (STATE) — COLORADO

Council Journal of the Legislative Assembly of the Territory of Colorado (Sixth Session, Dec. 3, 1866-Jan. 11, 1867). (Central City, 1867).

House Journal of the Legislative Assembly of the Territory of Colorado (Sixth Session, Dec. 3, 1866-Jan. 11, 1867). (Central City, 1867).

House Journal of the Legislative Assembly of the Territory of Colorado (Seventh Session, Dec. 2, 1867-Jan. 10, 1868). (Central City, 1868).

Session Laws of Colorado
(First Session, Sept. 9, 1861-Nov. 8, 1861). (Denver, 1861).

State Agricultural College.
Bulletin No. 44. (Technical Series No. 4). (Fort Collins, March, 1898).

BOOKS AND PAMPHLETS

Abdill, George B.
Pacific Slope Railroads from 1854 to 1900. Seattle, 1959.

Adams, Henry.
The Education of Henry Adams. New York, 1931.

Alter, J. Cecil.
Jim Bridger. Norman, Oklahoma, 1967.

Anderson, George L.
Kansas West. San Marino, California, 1963.

Athearn, Robert G.
Union Pacific Country. Chicago, 1971.

Baedeker, Karl, et al., compilers.
Switzerland and the Adjacent Portions of Italy, Savoy and Tyrol: Handbook for Travelers (English language edition). Leipzig, 1913.

Bailey, Alfred M., and Robert J. Niedrach.
Birds of Colorado. 2 volumes, Denver, 1965.
Pictorial Checklist of Colorado Birds. Denver, 1967.

Bancroft, Hubert Howe.
Works (Volume XXI, *Washington, Idaho, and Montana*). San Francisco, 1890.

Barry, Louise.
The Beginning of the West: Annals of the Kansas Gateway . . . Topeka, 1972.

Bashor, Belva Turner.
Early Berthoud: A History of the Town. Completed by Jodie Bashor Hanson and Helen McCarty Fickel. Fort Collins, Colorado, 1976.

Baskin, O.L. & Company.
History of Clear Creek and Boulder Valleys, Colorado. Chicago, 1880.
History of the City of Denver, Arapahoe County and Colorado. 2 vols. Chicago, 1880.

Beal, Merrill D.
Intermountain Railroads: Standard and Narrow Gauge. Caldwell, Idaho, 1962.

Berthoud, Edward L.
  Birds: Their Geological History, Migration and Uses. Golden, Colorado, 1887.
  The Boundaries of Louisiana. Golden, Colorado, 1897.
  Colorado Central R.R. "Itinerary," 1873 and 1874. Sketches, Scenery, etc., of
    the Rocky Mountains. St. Louis, 1873.
  The Ice Age and Pliocene Man. N.p., n.d.
  *A Table of Cubic Yards Corresponding to Areas from 1 to 1,000 for 100 feet in
    Length.* Golden, Colorado, 1889.
  compiler. *Jefferson County, Colorado: A Statistical Review of its Agricultural,
    Mining, Manufacturing and Pastorial Resources, from Official and Other
    Documentary Sources.* Golden City, Colorado, 1868.

Black, Robert C., III.
  Island in the Rockies: The History of Grand County, Colorado, to 1930. Boulder,
    Colorado, 1969.

Blake, J.A., publisher.
  Colorado Business Directory and Annual Register (for 1875-1878, inclusive).
    Denver, 1875-1878 (inclusive).

Bliss, John Homer, compiler.
  Genealogy of the Bliss Family in America . . . Boston, 1881.

Boatner, Mark May, III, compiler.
  The Civil War Dictionary. New York, 1959.

Breck, Allen DuPont.
  The Episcopal Church in Colorado, 1860-1963. Denver, 1963.

Broad, R.J.
  When Golden Was the Capital. Golden, Colorado, n.d.

Burt, Silas W., and Edward L. Berthoud.
  The Rocky Mountain Gold Regions, etc. Denver, 1861.

Business Directory, Montgomery and Fulton Counties, N.Y. (1869-70). N.p.,
  n.d.

Byers, William N., editor.
  Encyclopedia of Biography and History of Colorado. Chicago, 1901.

Collier, Edward A.
  A History of Old Kinderhook. New York, 1914.

Colorado Railroad Museum. *Colorado Rail Annual, No. 15.* Golden, Colorado,
  1981.

Colorado State Business Directory. N.p., 1883ff.

Combs, Barry B.
Westward to Promontory . . . New York, 1969.

Crocker, H.S., & Company, publisher.
McKenney's Business Directory of the Principal Towns of Utah, Wyoming, Colorado and Nebraska (for 1882). N.p., n.d.

Davis, E.O., compiler.
The First Five Years of the Railroad Era in Colorado. Denver, 1948.

Denver City Directory. (Various issues).

Doggett's New-York City Directory (1842/3-1845/6 inclusive). New York, 1843-1845, inclusive.

Drago, Harry Sinclair.
Canal Days in America: The History and Romance of Old Towpaths and Waterways. New York, 1972.

Encyclopedia Americana. International edition, 30 volumes, New York, 1964.

Feary, Thomas H., compiler.
Union College Alumni in th Civil War, 1861-1865. Schenectady, New York, 1915.

Federal Writers Project. *Kansas: A Guide to the Sunflower State.* New York, 1939.

Fitzpatrick, Lillian L., compiler.
Nebraska Place Names. Lincoln, 1964.

Fleming, Howard.
Narrow Gauge Railways in America. 2nd edition, Philadelphia, 1876.

Foothills Genealogical Society of Colorado. *Collections.* Lakewood, Colorado, 1984.

Frazer, Robert W.
Forts of the West. Norman, Oklahoma, 1965.

Gaeddert, G. Raymond.
The Birth of Kansas. Philadelphia, 1974.

Gazetteer Publishing Company. *Colorado State Business Directory (1908).* Denver, 1908.

Gibson, A.M.
The Kickapoos: Lords of the Middle Border. Norman, Oklahoma, 1963.

Goodrich, Carter, editor.
Canals and American Economic Development. New York, 1961.

Grant, Ulysses S.
Personal Memoirs of U.S. Grant. 2nd edition, 2 volumes, New York, 1895.

Greene, Nelson.
The Story of Old Fort Plain and the Middle Mohawk Valley. Fort Plain, New
York, 1915.
Fort Plain-Nelliston History. Fort Plain, New York, 1947.

Grodinsky, Julius.
Jay Gould: His Business Career, 1867-1892. Philadelphia, 1957.

Hafen, LeRoy R., editor.
*Colorado and Its People: A Narrative and Topical History of the Centennial
State.* 4 volumes, New York, 1948.
The Overland Mail, 1849-1869. Cleveland, Ohio, 1926.

Hall, Frank.
History of the State of Colorado. 4 volumes, Chicago, 1889-1895.

Harlow, Alvin F.
The Road of the Century: The Story of the New York Central. New York, 1947.

Harrison, Louise C.
Empire and the Berthoud Pass. Denver, 1964.

Hauck, Cornelius.
Narrow Gauge to Central City and Silver Plume. Golden, Colorado, 1972.

Heiss, W., and R.T. Mayhill, editors.
The Census of the Territory of Kansas, February, 1855. Knightstown, IN, 1967.

Hislop, Codman.
Eliphalet Nott. Middletown, Connecticut, 1971.

James, Edwin.
*Account of an Expedition from Pittsburgh to the Rocky Mountains Performed in
the Years of 1819, 1820.* 3 volumes, London, 1823.

Johnson, Allen, Dumas Malone, et al., editors.
Dictionary of American Biography. 22 volumes and supplements, New York,
1946-.)

Johnson, Robert Underwood, and Clarence Cough Beal, editors.
Battles and Leaders of the Civil War. 4 volumes, New York, 1884-1888.

Kemble, John Haskell.
The Panama Route, 1848-1869. Berkeley, California, 1943.

Kerby, Robert Lee.
The Confederate Invasion of New Mexico and Arizona, 1861-1862. Los Angeles, 1958.

Kimball, George M., and Louis E. Slingerland, compilers.
Illustrated Golden and Vicinity. Golden, Colorado, 1902.

Leavenworth, Pawnee & Western Railroad Company, compiler.
The Charters of the Leavenworth, Pawnee & Western Railroad Company (and Kansas Laws Affecting the Same). New York, 1864.

Lewis, Lloyd.
Captain Sam Grant. Boston, 1950.

Le Massena, R.A.
Colorado's Mountain Railroads. Volume V, Golden, Colorado, 1966.

Longworth, Thomas.
Longworth's American Almanac, New York Register and City Directory (issues for 1830/1 to 1842/3, inclusive). New York, 1830-1842, inclusive.

Lupo, Ruth V.
Waymarks in Nelliston, New York, 1878-1978. Nelliston, New York, 1978.

Miller, Francis Trevelyan, et al.
Photographic History of the Civil War. 10 volumes, New York, 1912.

Modelski, Andrew M., compiler.
Railroad Maps of the United States, etc. Washington, 1975.

Monaghan, Jay.
Civil War on the Western Border, 1854-1865. Boston, 1955.

Moore, H. Miles.
Early History of Leavenworth, City and County. Leavenworth, Kansas, 1906.

Morgan, Jesse R.
A World School: The Colorado School of Mines. Denver, 1955.

Morison, Samuel Eliot.
The European Discovery of America: The Northern Voyages. New York, 1971.

Nankivel, John H.
History of Military Organizations of the State of Colorado, 1860-1935. Denver, 1935.

National Cyclopaedia of American Biography. 52 volumes, New York, 1898-1970.

Nevins, Allan.
Hamilton Fish: The Inner History of the Grant Administration. New York, 1936.

Niedrach, Robert J., and Robert B. Rockwell.
The Birds of Denver and Mountain Parks. Denver, 1959.

Ormes, Robert M.
Railroads and the Rockies: A Record of Lines in and near Colorado. Denver, 1963.

Otis, F.N.
Illustrated History of the Panama Railroad. Pasadena, California, 1971.

Perkins, J.R.
Trails, Rails and War: The Life of General G.M. Dodge. Indianapolis, 1929.

Quiett, Glenn Chesney.
They Built the West: An Epic of Rails and Cities. New York, 1934.

Rawley, James A.
Race and Politics: "Bleeding Kansas" and the Coming of the Civil War. Philadelphia, 1969.

Raymond, Andrew Van Vranken.
Union University: Its History, Influence, Characteristics and Equipment. 3 volumes, New York, 1907.

Rebel Invasion of Missouri and Kansas and the Campaign of the Army of the Border against Sterling Price. Chicago, 1865.

Reeves, Thomas C.
Gentleman Boss: The Life of Chester Alan Arthur. New York, 1975.

Report of the Organization of the Union Pacific R.R. Co. New York, 1864.

Richardson, Ernest Cushing, and Anson Ely Morse, compilers.
Writings on American History. Princeton, New Jersey, 1904.

Riestop, J.-B., compiler.
The Armorial General. 2 volumes, Baltimore, 1965.

Riestop, J.-B., V. Rolland, and H.V. Rolland, compilers. *Illustrations to the Armorial General.* 2 volumes, Baltimore, 1967.

Schott, Joseph L.
Rails Across Panama: The Story of the Building of the Panama Railroad, 1849-1855. Indianapolis, 1967.

Sclater, W.L.
Birds of Colorado. London, 1912.

Seward, Frederick W.
Reminiscences of a War-Time Statesman and Diplomat, 1830-1915. New York, 1916.

Simon, John Y., Editor.
Papers of U.S. Grant. 5 volumes, Carbondale, Illinois, 1967-1973.

Spence, Clark C.
Territorial Politics and Government in Montana, 1864-1889. Urbana, Illinois, 1975.

Sherman, William T.
Memoirs of General William T. Sherman. 2 volumes, New York, 1891.

State Business Directory of Colorado (for 1881). N.p., n.d.

Stover, John F.
Iron Road to the West: American Railroads in the 1850s. New York, 1878.
American Railroads. Chicago, 1962.

Todd, Frederick P., et al.
American Military Equipage, 1851-1872. 3 volumes, Westbrook, Connecticut, 1978.

Utley, Robert M.
Frontiersman in Blue: The United States Army and the Indian, 1848-1865. New York, 1967.

The War of the Rebellion: The Official Records of the Union and Confederate Armies. 128 volumes, Washington, 1880-1901.

Warner, Ezra J.
Generals in Blue. Baton Rouge, 1964.

Weber, Thomas.
The Northern Railroads in the Civil War, 1861-1865. New York, 1952.

Wharton, Junis E.
History of the City of Denver from its Earliest Settlement to the Present Time. Denver, 1866.

Wilkins, Tivis E., compiler.
Colorado Railroads: Chronological Development. Boulder, Colorado, 1974.

Williams, Ellen.
Three Years and a Half in the Army; or, History of the Second Colorado. New York, 1885.

Zornow, William Frank.
Kansas: A History of the Jayhawk State. Norman, Oklahoma, 1957.

PERIODICALS

American Journal of Science.
American Naturalist.
Botanical Gazette.
Bulletins. Agricultural College of Colorado, Fort Collins.
Bulletin of the Nuttall Ornithological Club.
Bulletin of the Railway and Locomotive Historical Society.
Collections, the Kansas State Historical Society.
Colorado Genealogist.
Colorado Magazine.
Colorado School of Mines Catalog.
Colorado School of Mines Quarterly.
Denver Westerners Monthly Roundup.
Idaho Yesterdays.
Indiana Magazine of History.
Kansas City Review of Science and Industry.
Kansas Historical Quarterly.
Mississippi Valley Historical Review.
Missouri Historical Review.
Montana: Magazine of Western History.
National Geographic Magazine.
Official Guide of the Railways.
Panama Canal Review.
Purple and Gold. (Official magazine of Chi Psi Fraternity.)
Real West.
Record of Proceedings of the Davenport Academy of Natural Sciences.
Saga.
Sister Republics.
Sons of Colorado.
Trail.
Transactions. (Kansas State Historical Society.)
Transactions of the Wisconsin Academy of Science, Arts and Letters.
Travelers' Official Guide of the Railways.

NEWSPAPERS

Colorado Miner (Georgetown)
Colorado Transcript (Golden)
Daily Herald (Helena, Montana)
Daily Independent (Helena, Montana)
Daily Journal of Commerce (Kansas City, Missouri)
Daily Miners' Register (Black Hawk)
Denver Post
Denver Republican
Denver Times
Denver Tribune
Denver Weekly Commonwealth
Golden Globe
Jefferson County Republican (Golden)
Leadville Daily Chronicle
Leavenworth (Kansas) Times
Missoula (Montana) Weekly Missoulian
Mountain City ("Jefferson") Gold Reporter
Mountain City Herald
Radii (Canajoharie, New York)
Rocky Mountain News Denver
Soldier's Letter (Regimental Organ, 2nd Colorado Volunteer Cavalry)
Western Mountaineer (Golden City)
Tripp, Julie and E. Dale Ogden, editors, "100 Years" Supplement of Colorado
    Daily Transcript, Golden, Colorado, 1959.

DISSERTATIONS

Napier, Rita G.
    "Squatter City: The Construction of a New Community in the American
    West, 1854-1861." Ph.D. dissertation, American University, 1976.
Turner, Wallace B.
    "Kentucky in a Decade of Change, 1850-1860." Ph.D. dissertation, Univer-
    sity of Kentucky, 1954.

UNPUBLISHED MANUSCRIPTS

Adams, Harry B.
"Short Biography of Edward Louis Berthoud." Berthoud Papers, Coloorado Historical Society, Denver.

Bromwell, Henrietta E., compiler.
"Fifty-niners' Directory: Colorado Argonauts of 1858-1859." 2 volumes, Denver Public Library.

Burt, Silas Wright.
"My Personal Reminiscences." New York Historical Society, New York.

Colorado Historical Society.
"The Exhibit Content Outline: Steps in Planning." Colorado Historical Society, Denver.

Daughters of the American Revolution (Lookout Mountain Chapter).
"History of Golden Notebooks." 2 volumes, Denver Public Library.

Denver Public Library, compiler.
"Legal Titles of Subdivisions in Adams, Arapahoe, Boulder, Denver, Jefferson Counties." Denver Public Library.

SCRAPBOOKS

Dawson Scrapbooks. Colorado Historical Society, Denver.

INDEX

A

Acequia, Colorado, 74
Alkali, Nebraska, 53
American Journal of Science, 109
Ames, Oakes and Oliver, 82
Arthur, Chester Alan, 6

B

Baldwin, James L., 11
Bear (Yampa) River, 34
Beaverhead Canyon, 95
Berthoud, Alexander Pierre, 2, 6, 89, 108
Berthoud, Charles Louis Henri, 2-4
Berthoud, Edward Louis, childhood, 2-5; college, 6-8; early work, 9-18; surveys in Kansas, 19-25; first Colorado ventures and the Berthoud Pass explorations, 26-38; Civil War service, 39-51; post-war and Union Pacific survey, 52-56; Colorado territorial politics, 57-61; Colorado Central Railroad

activities, 63-87; subsequent surveys, 90-103; other business activites, 103-108; death of Helen, 109; later years and writings, 111-121; death, 122-123
Berthoud, Emilie, 2
Berthoud, Ernest, 4
Berthoud, Frederic Stephen, 2, 25
Berthoud, Helen Samaria Ferrell, marriage, 21; in Kansas, 24; in Golden, 26, 28; mother's death, 43; Civil War experiences, 47; return to Golden, 53-54; entertains legislature, 58; greets Berthoud on return from Montana, 95; Golden social activities, 103; death, 109
Berthoud, Margaret Haupt, 2
Berthoud, Margaret, 2
Berthoud, Matilde, 2, 123
Berthoud, Nicholas, 4
Berthoud, Colorado, 8586
Berthoud Pass, exploration, 32; as more direct route west from Denver, 37; suggested as Union Pacific route, 55-56; re-survey, 99

ABOUT THE AUTHOR

Railroad historian Robert C. Black III is best known for his seminal work, *The Railroads of the Confederacy*, which has remained the definitive study of the South's railroad network since its 1952 publication. Although born in New York City, Dr. Black has spent more than half of his life in Colorado, making many journeys across Edward Berthoud's pass between his Denver home and his ranch in Middle Park. He graduated from Williams College in Williamstown, Massachusetts, in 1937 and received an M.A. in history from the University of Denver and a Ph.D. in history from Columbia University. Dr. Black's army service during World War II as a rail transportation officer in Atlanta stimulated his railroad interests and led to his study of Confederate railroads. He has taught American history at Trinity College in Hartford, Connecticut, and at Colorado Women's College in Denver. Other published works include *The Younger John Winthrop*, a study of an early leader of Connecticut, and *Island in the Rockies: The Pioneer Era of Grand County, Colorado*, which is that area beyond Berthoud Pass known as Middle Park. Among his many avocations, Dr. Black counts ornithology, geography, travel, astronomy, and of course railroads.

Cordillera Press

AUGUSTA TABOR A Pioneering Woman
Betty Moynihan
160 Pages, Photos, (6 x 9), ISBN: 0-917895-23-1, Softcover, $7.95

COLORADO PROFILES Men and Women Who Shaped the Centennial State
John H. Monnett and Michael McCarthy
340 Pages, Photos, (6 x 9), ISBN: 0-917895-19-3, Softcover, $14.95

**GUIDE TO HISTORIC
DURANGO & SILVERTON**
Duane A. Smith
48 Pages, Photos, Maps, (7½ x 9), ISBN: 0-917895-16-6, Softcover, $4.95

**GUIDE TO HISTORIC
CENTRAL CITY & BLACK HAWK**
Sarah J. Pearce and Christine Pfaff
48 Pages, Photos, Maps, (7½ x 9), ISBN: 0-917895-15-0, Softcover, $4.95

**GUIDE TO
THE GEORGETOWN-SILVER PLUME HISTORIC DISTRICT**
48 Pages, Photos, Maps, (7½ x 9), ISBN: 0-917895-08-8, Softcover, $4.95

ROOF OF THE ROCKIES A History of Colorado Mountaineering
William M. Bueler
264 Pages, Photos, Maps, (5½ x 8½), ISBN: 0-917895-06-1, Softcover, $12.95

SKI TRACKS IN THE ROCKIES A Century of Colorado Skiing
Abbott Fay
100 Pages, Photos, (8½ x 10½), ISBN: 0-917895-02-9, Softcover, $10.95